Alberto Iacovoni

Game Zone
Playgrounds between Virtual Scenarios and Reality

Translation into English by Gail McDowell

A CIP catalogue record for this book is available from the Library of Congress, Washington D.C., USA.

Deutsche Bibliothek Cataloging-in-Publication Data

Bibliographic information published by Die Deutsche Bibliothek
Die Deutsche Bibliothek lists this publication in the Deutsche Nationalbibliografie; detailed bibliographic data is available in the Internet at <http://dnb.ddb.de>.

This work is subject to copyright. All rights are reserved, whether the whole or part of the material is concerned, specifically the rights of translation, reprinting, re-use of illustrations, recitation, broadcasting, reproduction on microfilms or in other ways, and storage in data banks. For any kind of use permission of the copyright owner must be obtained.

Original edition:
Game Zone (Universale di Architettura, collana fondata da Bruno Zevi; La Rivoluzione Informatica, sezione diretta da Antonino Saggio).
© 2004 Testo & Immagine, Turin

© 2004 Birkhäuser – Publishers for Architecture, P.O. Box 133, CH-4010 Basel, Switzerland.
Part of Springer Science+Business Media Publishing Group.
Printed on acid-free paper produced from chlorine-free pulp. TCF ∞
Printed in Italy
ISBN 3-7643-0151-1

9 8 7 6 5 4 3 2 1   http://www.birkhauser.ch

Contents

00: intro	6
01: play	8
: what shall we play	8
: let's pretend	9
: is it a children's game	11
: what part do we play?	12
: and the rules?	12
: and the playground?	15
02: playgrounds	19
playground 01: the game of points of view	20
playground 02: the game of the body in space	28
playground 03: the game invades the city	35
playground 04: the play city	43
playground 05: the game of instant architecture	54
playground 06: invaders of space	62
03: playscape	78
04: playlist	89

I would like to express my thanks and my gratitude first of all to Nino Saggio, for having given me the opportunity and the freedom to write this book, to the tireless and enthusiastic Luca Galofaro, to all those who partake in my daily play, Luca, Massimo and Ketty of ma0, to all the Stalkers, to Francesco (Piccio) Careri in particular, to my guide in the land of electronic games Jaime D'Alessandro, and to those who, even with a few words, allowed criticism to sift downwards and suggestions to rise, like Marco Brizzi and Stefano Mirti.
A particularly affectionate thank you to Andrea and Francesca, whose hospitality enabled a large portion of these pages to be written, to my mother, because without her nothing would have been possible, and to my favorite play companion, Pia.

Depending on what you're looking for, choose a district, a city that is more or less densely populated, a street that is more or less animated. Build a house. Furnish it. Get the most out of its decoration and its surroundings. Choose the season of the year and the time of day. Bring together the most suitable people, the records and the wines and spirits that are most appropriate. The illumination and the conversation will, of course, have to be suitable to the circumstances, like the climate or your memories. If you haven't made any mistakes in your calculations, the result should satisfy you. (Communicate the results to the editors.)

(Potlatch 96, p. 15)

00: intro

The relationships between architecture and play have been multiplying and expanding throughout the entire last century up to today, in such a multiplicity of different contexts and situations that it has become indispensable to clarify – first of all, and at least etymologically – what we mean by play, but also what we mean by *architecture*.

From the many games that use space as a raw material – hide-and-seek, for example – all the way to real playgrounds, areas that are planned exclusively for playing in, to the theme parks that over the last thirty years have assumed the dimensions of true cities, all the way to the multitude of unusual and unpredictable spaces that are produced by the videogame industry at an amazing rate, from the New Babylon Constant imagined, to the urban games of the 1960's, and up to the interactive spaces of our games today, the nature of the relationship between these two terms has become so variable that we must cut, choose a path, and not only because of the space at our disposal – this book – as opposed to the enormity of the task. Above all, there is a guideline that re-emerges from the folds of history, like a seam that unites two strips of different cloth, along which the relationship between architecture and play has developed a meaning that is much more than just instrumental – play like any other function of architecture. It has founded practices and projects that strove to – or that could and can – radically change the relationship between man and space.

But it's hard enough to say exactly what games are and what architecture is, not just because of the vagueness that is innate in these two terms. The first is used to name attitudes and actions by facts and values that incorporate antitheses, the other is an accommodating term to indicate a professional and academic specific that is at the mercy of the complexities of the territories it must confront itself with. But – and not by chance – just when the ties between an aptitude for play and the construction of a space are strongest, these two terms seem to become all-comprehensive, they don't accept limitations, they expand into every manifestation of collective life. *Play must invade life as a whole*, the Situationists (IS 94) decreed, *everything is architecture*, Hollein revealed… The fact is that this interweaving was supported – and we wonder if this can still be the case today - by the will to eliminate the separation between the construction of a project and true life, between ideology and the production of relations, a *concrete utopia* that would soon be realized through play…

To understand the deep reasons behind this interweaving will help us to both prune and demystify, to consciously exclude architecture that was built specifically for games and perhaps include others in which we reserve the right to glimpse a sincere sensibility toward play. Others will be ignored, not only because of an objective inability on the author's part to fill the unexplored zones of such a vast territory – but also simply for the sake of classification, since this book was written by an architect who believes – hopes – he has at his disposal a few true and specific instruments with which to intervene on the territory. And his declared objective is to highlight potentialities and instruments with an aptitude toward play in architecture.

We will be extremely indulgent and full of expectations with regard to the notion of *architecture*, as Gilles Ivain wrote:

> Architecture is the simplest way to articulate time and space, to mold reality, to let people dream. It isn't just plastic articulation and molding, an expression of fleeting beauty. But rather, influential modulation that is inscribed in the eternal curve of human desires and progress in the realization of these desires. The architecture of tomorrow will therefore be a way to modify the present conceptions of time and space. It will be a means of knowledge and a means of action. (IS 94)

On the other hand, we will be very exacting with regard to *play*, the significant limit and dividing line of this entire research, and we will ask ourselves first of all the following question: *What game shall we play?*

01: play

: what shall we play?

Every morning, some children go out without anxiety. Everything is near, the worst material conditions are excellent. The woods are white or black, they will never sleep there. (Sacks 98)

It is the first question we must answer in this research, but it was also the first question we spontaneously asked each other when we were small and someone our age would offer himself as a companion in a new adventure: *what shall we play?* This question presses for an agreement, the choice of a field and the rules, in short, the definition of a *reference framework* within which to interact. Without this framework we wouldn't know what to expect, since a game can be, can become, a thousand different plays.

Few other words have the same capacity as *play* to signify such a vast body of activities while yet maintaining a specificity of meaning. As short as the attention span of a child or as endless and complex as the life of a character in a role-playing game; as highly serious as a *game theory* mathematical model used by military strategists or as pithy and evanescent as *nonsense*. So poor that it only takes a bit of imagination to start playing, as in hide-and-seek,

where the material needed to play is no more than the surrounding space, or as rich and complex in its preparation, requiring time, money and capabilities worthy of a Hollywood set, as a contemporary *videogame*. As disinterested as a word game or as totally *functional* as those in which organizational experts involve company managers to increase creativity and productivity. Each one of these activities is, therefore, undeniably play, not to mention the fact that people are trying to convince us that *play* also means consuming the latest creations of the electronics industry – to turn our vacations into multimedia art, get drunk or even make love – hey, *play* is also one of the specialties of a well-known producer of condoms!

: let's pretend…

Every game combines different components in a precarious equilibrium which safeguards its course, becoming its motive power, as it were. Caillois, one of the authors who classified this activity which is so hard to define, has identified four different ones: *alea*, a characteristic of all those games in which one tries one's luck; *agon*, which encourages competition and excellence; *ilynx*, which is the characteristic component of every game in which the pleasure is to be found in dizziness and loss of orienta-

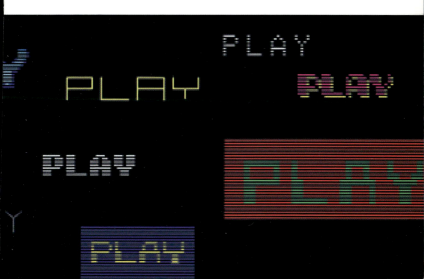

tion, like in a labyrinth, or *bungee jumping*; and lastly, *mimicry*, the driving force behind all those games that are mainly built on the simulation of a more or less imaginary reality.

These, and perhaps other, components sometimes interweave inextricably – for example, how can you tell alea from argon in a card game, where the objective is to win by ably administering fate? They create scenarios and situations that are sometimes so distant from each other, in their dynamics and in the emotions they stimulate, that one wonders how can they can be defined by one word, by just one concept. The answer is in the very nature of the game, in its most characteristic and pervasive power: to play is first of all *in-ludere*, literally "to enter into the game" but it is also "illusion", to construct each time a new *in-lusio*, the illusion of a possible reality, of a separate world with different rules from those which, sometimes unfortunately, we observe during most of our waking hours.

The passion for playing, therefore, is a result of its ability to be a free and knowing *diversion* from the beaten path, a moment of *re-creation* of parallel universes in which we are freed of identity, rules of cause and effect, physical and material bonds and the rigidity of the world we live in. It is the precursor of a *virtual* reality without the use of technology, in which we can experience a thousand different games, and a thousand different lives.

Our first answer to the question *what shall we play*, if we weren't dealing with codified and recognized games but had to invent a new world, was *let's pretend that…*: the definition of a fictitious scenario, an open door onto entire, imaginary landscapes to be entered in the knowledge that, by voluntarily obeying the rules in force beyond that limit, we were acquiring an unpredictable freedom in which the game becomes experience, adventure, narration…

> Anon, to sudden silence won
> In fancy they pursue
> The dream-child moving through a land
> Of wonders wild and new,
> In friendly chat with bird or beast –
> And half believe it's true.
> (l. Carroll, *Lewis Carroll, Alice's Adventures in Wonderland and Through the Looking Glass*)

: is it a children's game?

This *land of wonders wild and new* where a *friendly chat with bird or beast* is a normal occurrence is a place that seems to change as one matures: from man's childhood, where "the absence of any known strictness leaves him with the prospective of many lives lived simultaneously", and the child "puts down roots into that illusion" and "wants to know nothing more than the momentary and extreme facility of every thing" (Breton 66) to adulthood, where, on the contrary, the word *illusion* becomes tainted with original sin because of its connotations of precariousness and futility – but, as Breton points out, there is nothing more precarious than the real world with its false promises of happiness – the games seems to evolve slowly into more codified and regulated forms that neutralize its power of *re-creation* of reality and *diversion* from the beaten path… But that very *absence of strictness* and that *extreme facility* of children's games, which continually produce "wild and new" lands, are the fundamental motors of a culture's evolution, not just in the sense of a *competitive* stimulus for excellence and, therefore, of the constant growth of a society's intellectual and artistic capabilities, as Huizinga (Huizinga 73) states, but as a free space in which people can change their point of view about the reality surrounding them, a reality which is viewed as unalterable, but is in fact only one of the *possible* worlds.

Playing, an activity of the young of every species, seems to extend all the way to adulthood as one progresses up the evolutionary scale, naturally following what Morin called the *youthfulization of the human species*, a phenomenon in which young people become the "carriers, within the class of men, of their pleasure in play, their affectivity, their many questions, their omnivorous curiosity", contributing to the "regression of stereotypical behavior (instinctual) that was innately programmed", thanks to their "extreme openness to the environment (natural and societal)" and "great plasticity and availability" (Morin 74) to dismantle and look with new and fertilely *ignorant* eyes at the world around them, and to continuously reconstruct it with that *extreme facility*, that total liberty to follow their own pleasure like a principle of truth, rather than the false objectives imposed by culture.

: what part do we play?

The message "this is a game", which players exchange more or less clearly, an enunciation of a preliminary agreement that is consciously and freely accepted, highlights a *behavioral framework* that spans every other framework with which culture topologically defines roles and limits, overlapping them like layers of onion skin. By means of games, discovering where the lines are that divide these layers, learning to cross them, we become children who are aware of the various types of behavioral categories (Bateson 96).

For this reason, the imaginary reality of games isn't *evasion* – a term which is perhaps appropriate to certain reified formats for games and travel we will deal with later, in which the imagination is eager to consume. Above all, it is the place where the separation from our "framework of reference" becomes the substantial premise for the formation of the *conscious* ("le jeu [...] comme l'ironie Kierkegaardienne, delivre la subjectivité (...) dès qu'un homme se saisit comme libre [...], son activité est de jeu" [Sartre 43]) and where crossing the limits society has drawn for us shows us how arbitrary the rules and the unwritten but tacitly obeyed conventions are. Rather than objects within a structured system, we become thinking subjects beyond the mirror, beyond the magic circle of a playground, where we can overturn our point of view, and finally question our role: "We want to live, says Pascal, in the idea of others, in an imaginary life and this is why we strive to appear. We ceaselessly work to embellish and conserve this imaginary being and we neglect the authentic one" (Vaneigem 67).

: and the rules?

Therefore: let's enter the game, let's leave reality behind, we look back and measure the distance that separates a temporary illusion from a permanent one, the great parlor game whose rules can only be questioned at a high price. And after eras of geological settling... we achieve a "freedom to play" that allows us to cross over behavioral categories and discover new roles. To avoid becoming a simple leave-taking – an absence – from the laws of rationality or from "that's how the world goes", maybe within the hyper-controlled circuits of organized "leisure", or, as Agamben wrote, the destruction of time and of experience within the permanent potlatch of Toyland (Agamben 79), or even simply the freedom to criticize the existing world, it must become an instrument of transformation and re-creation of a world…

The demarcation line between game and game that we are looking for, therefore, cannot be found in the *in-lusio*, which is a part of every game and is the necessary but not self-sufficient condition for games to become creative. Rather, it is built entirely on the relations between the two substantial components which entwine in its becoming, which transform it into a narrative event, an experience: *play* and *game*.

What has been purposefully omitted, to this point, in this search for values that are common to every game, is the fact that Italian, as well as other languages like German and Dutch, use two *homonyms* to denote two extremely different concepts, which correspond in English to two very distinct terms, as Umberto Eco notes in the preface to the Italian edition of *Homo Ludens* (Eco 73):

> The English word *game* stresses the *aspect of competence*, of a group of rules that are known and recognized. […] For instance, the *Games Theory*, when one wants to underline the intention of studying the rules and the combinations that are permitted. Tennis, poker, golf are *games*: systems of rules, schema of action, combinatorial matrices of possible moves. "To play the game" means "to follow the rules." There is an abstract subject, a *game*, and then there is concrete behavior, a *performance*, a *play*. *To play* is "to take part in a game."

We are completely lost, without any reference points or dialectical elements, in a world of playthings without rules, where the only principle of action seems to be the immediacy of pleasure, of play. On the contrary, in a hyper-regulated game, where the players' every move is predicted and controlled – in any playground – our experience becomes an obligatory pathway, a guided tour, the passive assumption of a reality that was prepackaged by others.

But between these two extremes there are an infinity of games in which the relationship between these two poles is unpredictably modulated, where playing is all in experiencing the limits, the pleasure – and the ability, when it is a competitive game – in knowing how to interpret, bypass and use them following one's own strategy… And at a certain point, somewhere between these two extremes, the *game* of our existence – within a *set of rules* made of prohibitions, conventions, impulses, inhibitions and an infinity of norms that are often obeyed but not always written – becomes so intricate and so nuanced that the importance of the *play*, or rather the performance and the improvisation, becomes fundamental in its capacity to continuously re-interpret and question the rules themselves.

At a convention in 1955, Gregory Bateson invited a group of scientists with fairly heterogeneous interests to discuss games. The declared objective was to "discover the processes by which living beings get themselves out of trouble on their own, freeing themselves from the rules of communication – the onionskin layers within which they are working."

In this group discussion, which continuously spanned the different branches of the speakers' knowledge as they tried to construct a definition of games from various points of view, Bateson came to the conclusion that *games* are every activity with hyper-simplified rules, which logically set forth what can and can't be done, and which, therefore, can be considered part of a defined, logical category, whereas *play* means those games in which the multiple levels that constitute our communication – since we normally use a language and a meta-language that are combined into a single embryonic process – cannot be separated. Every move of the game can also be a proposal to change the rules and therefore to manage to "get oneself out of trouble", moving "toward new rules and new philosophies" (Bateson 96). And in one of those illuminating dialogs between father and daughter in *Metalogues* (Bateson 77) we are told that play is life itself, "a game whose aim is to discover the rules, rules that are always changing and that can never be discovered."

There we have it: if life is a game whose aim is to discover the rules, a space is created in which a play can be activated to try out various moves to change them, operating within that "zone of uncertainty between brain and environment" which "is also the zone of uncertainty between subjectivity and objectivity, between the imaginary and reality" (Morin 74).

: and the playground?

There is a part of the rules of every game that needs room, that becomes a *playground*, architecture whose limits represent prohibitions and opportunities for the player, who is thus transformed into an *inhabitant*.

These spaces, too, follow the infinite modulations of the game: the playground is inexistent, or almost so, in card games; it is simple and geometric in a few board games; but it can permit a high degree of complexity, it can be as real as a Wisconsin forest where company managers are abandoned for *survival training*, or it can be left up to improvisation like in a game of hide-and-seek. Playgrounds are the visible form of a system of rules, the architecture which gives space to the players' performances.

The spaces in which the great social game of our cities is continuously developing are the playground on which the architect intervenes, raising boundaries, opening entrances, creating interfaces, limiting public and private spaces, foreseeing possible actions and movements on the part of the inhabitants, giving form to a set of written rules. But he also has the power to question them, to propose new ones.

The spaces where the game of reality is taking place are complex spaces, "heterogeneous and interconnected spaces where men continuously produce, transform and build, sentimental, aesthetic, social and historic spaces, spaces with meaning, in general" (Serres 72).

They are "ground" (as in play-) according to the meaning that physicists give to a force field, in constant transformation – deformation – under the pressure of the forces that cross it, a spatial form of the constant redefinition of the rules which is the incessant play of our existence.

If architecture wants to be that field, far from the sterile self-referencing of the rigid and simplified game of the discipline and the dogmatic amplification of productive dynamics, remaining within reality without dissolving into the simulation of an inexistent spontaneity, it must become a continuous *play*, around and against its own rules. It must extend itself to the multiple layers of man's space, cross them and produce *illusions* of possible worlds, it must become "a means to modify the present conditions of space and time, […] an instrument of knowledge and a means of action." (IS 94)

Since it would be impossible to tell the history of play spaces, since it would involve so many stories that are often parallel and with no relation to one another at all, this text will try to describe a landscape, crossing those places where an aptitude for games, declared or undeclared, finds concrete form in the spaces that can produce possible worlds, *virtual* worlds, which can change our relationships with space, with those around us, with ourselves.

This exploration will move along clues that were given in the first chapter, which create the hypothesis of a crime – which is subversive to a certain extent – that will have to be proven in the field, or rather on the playgrounds. They will be put in order according to an imaginary scale of the technological complexity that is needed to build them, in a path that starts and ends up again in the imaginary world.

Each one of these playgrounds has its own specific scale of intervention, its special instruments for constructing a play space; it is architecture in the sense that every modification of living space is architecture, and it is a place where theories, projects and realizations share a common, operative method.

The first playground is that of the eye, where all one has to do is change one's point of view to construct whole new cities; the second deals with the body, and the significant relationships that it establishes with space; the third exports space from the city to other bodies, urban games which mark the times and the places of daily life, mixing roles and hierarchies; the fourth playground finds its most complete and anticipatory expression in Constant's *New Babylon* and includes all the architecture that has tried to combine the solidity of the constructed with the fluidity of the real, integrating new and old technologies; the fifth is a playground where physical ties of architectonic space evaporate in the multi-sensorial experience produced by technology; the sixth and last is that enormous, vast, highly populated playground of videogames, the multiple place in which millions of people not only spend an increasing part of their time, but in which they construct relationships, they invent new roles, break rules.

Within these playgrounds, constructed with the fragments of those radical experiences which, for the first time, gave the individual the power to create his own space, a series of specific reports

about projects and contemporary realizations offer the reader the opportunity to confront the potential and the limits of experiences that are distant in time, like trying to imagine what one person would have done with the technology that was available to another, or what the other would have done with the revolutionary tensions of the first…

This is a sort of architectonic *Frankenstein*, hybrid, impure, unpredictable, perhaps too lightweight for some or, on the contrary, too inappropriately political for others. Every playground is a minimal manual, a small book of instructions shaped like a *collage*, like the images in which we will find much play-related architecture, "the integration of present or past productions in a construction that is superior to the environment," (IS 94) a possible *playscape*. Therefore beware: "This work is entirely composed of prefabricated elements" (Debord, Jorn 59).

02: playgrounds

The term *playground* generally indicates the areas that are set aside in gardens and urban parks for children to play in: delimited, controlled spaces that are protected from the intrusion of the adult world by a high rail fence, often they contain nothing more than a few pieces that have been ordered from a catalog with the certainty that, just like the furnishings of a house must inevitably include tables, chairs, couches, armchairs, etc., a play area necessarily has to have slides, swings, rocking horses, and the like.

The desolation of these playgrounds is the mirror image of a society which leaves very little space to playing, unless it is behind a fence, beyond the box office of a theme park, imprisoned and neutralized within the confines of "free time".

Each one of the following playgrounds, on the other hand, solicits the tearing down of that fence, as well as respect for the most profound reason that children play: life is discovery, dreams, adventure.

playground 01
Ceci n'est pas un pipe: The Game of Points of View

This playground is a strange place, simultaneously familiar and unknown. It is the beginning of a low-cost adventure, which we enter like the explorers of a new world. But actually it is nothing more than the world we live in every day, which we will traverse like discoverers after having dismantled it, turned it upside down, and recomposed it according to our will and desire.

This playground is everywhere, in the streets of our city like in the intimate folds of home life, it is a space of the possible that is created each time – and with an elementary and simple act, for pure pleasure or to spark a revolution – we are willing to *change our point of view*.

This is *in-lusio* in its purest state, which transforms objects, makes space, in the blink of an eye…

Children are well acquainted with the key to this realm, at an

ma0 , glove, 2002

age when the borderline between illusion and reality is still, as Breton tells us, so indistinct that it can be crossed unconsciously, "with the extreme ease of every thing". But for adults, in an era in which that borderline has become a barrier which, surprisingly, we don't even notice anymore, it has become necessary to enter this realm with an act – simple but radical – of voluntary forgetfulness, which can take us back in time and consciousness to a moment when objects around us didn't have a definite meaning yet, when reality had yet to be structured into a group of things representing rules, functions, values.

> "And what's this?" I asked, lifting a glove.
> "A continuous surface, wrapped around itself. Equipped with five hollow extensions, if one may put it that way."
> Later, he slipped it on by chance. "My God!" he exclaimed, "It's a glove!" This is like Lanuti, a patient of Kurt Goldstein, who could only recognize objects if he tried to put them to their intended purpose."

ma0, bottle, 2003.

The scene is the following: a neurologist visits a patient who is affected by a strange ailment – with increasing frequency, he not only doesn't recognize the faces of the people he knows, "but he even sees them where they aren't: like Mr. Magoo, when walking on the street he would affectionately pat water hydrants and parking meters, mistaking them for children's heads; he would speak nicely to furniture knobs and would be surprised when he didn't receive an answer" (Sacks 98).

This story, like many others in the same book, describes an altered state of perception, and in particular a sort of visual agnosia. This is the pathological analogy of a projected act that is necessary if one wants to enter the first playground: a vacuum in which meaning disappears and becomes, in fact, the virgin territory in which to explore its forms, its uses, its meaning. The ensuing *destruction of the objects* produces a tabula rasa on which a new universe of relationships can be constructed.

Changing one's point of view is a game that gives the individual back the power of renaming things, freeing him "from the formal structures that transmit sensations and actions, conditioning and repressing him in the same way as moral and behavioral structures" (Toraldo di Francia 2001). It is a game that passes through an act of negation, loss, estrangement, beyond which the reality surrounding us is transformed into a series of pieces, pawns, bricks, fragments to be freely used as we recompose them into a constellation with a different meaning. The rule, if we must indicate one, is that you play with what there is.

Like a collage, where nothing can be glued together if first you haven't used a pair of scissors to cut the chosen figures out of their context, there are two distinct yet inseparable operations of *decontextualization and recontextualization* (Andreotti 96) of the pre-existing elements, which form an instrument that is both creative and critical. Critical because it stimulates a reflection on and knowledge of the existing reality, creative because it can result in its being turned totally upside down, using very few means, and with limited technical and artistic ability. This playground is rightfully one of the favorite of last century's avant-garde ("the low cost of its products is the heavy artillery with which all the Chinese walls of intelligence are breached" [IS 94]), which used it to break down not just the meaning of the objects, but the functionalist myth of the coincidence between form and function:

> As Baudrillard notes, the surrealist object is born in the same era as the functional object, as its mockery, its transgression: "The Bauhaus synthesis of form and function, of beauty and usefulness, of art and technique, is turned upside down by the hybrid game of the surrealists, which places itself between the figure of the object and that of man, between function and desire." (Bandini 99)

The most simple and immediate way to create this playground, so rapid it is called *ready-made*, is to take an object and turn it upside down and, following the dadaist example, transform it from a urinal into a *fountain*, instantly and elementarily dissolving the ties that bind that object with its inseparable form, whose meaning is commonly accepted and incorporated in the value of its use.

This simple negation of primary identity between form and value of use opens the way to the distortion of the symbolic and iconic qualities which society and the market (publicity, the media, culture) have assigned to each object, turning them into *merchandise* that can incorporate images of lifestyles and models of behavior. It is the strategy of the Situationists, who propose *détournement* to integrate "past or present art productions into a superior environmental construction" (IS 94). Or of various exponents of that multi-form phenomenon called "radical architecture" which, from inside the world of production, boldly mix *pop* icons and ritual forms in projects where *design* is "the vehicle of an image of individual freedom, of a system that foresees and permits dissimilar, alternative and eccentric behavior" and "the domestic landscape," no longer based on anachronistic value scales, becomes "the ideal space of individual freedom" (Orlandoni, Vallino 77).

But this playground's field of action isn't limited to the object and the construction of habitats: it goes well beyond, to the territory, the city, where changing one's point of view is the first step toward overcoming norms and behavior – in other words, the "rules" that are written in the form/function of the space of collective living. Changing one's point of view about collective space which on the one hand "should be homogeneous, open to reasonable, authorized or commanded actions, and on the other, is loaded with the prohibitions of hidden qualities, of favorable and unfavorable situations, for the individual and groups" (Lefebvre 81),

STALKER, *TOUR OF ROME*, 1995

The Actual Territories. *They constitute the negative of the constructed city, interstitial and peripheral areas, spaces that have been abandoned or that are being transformed. They are the areas of repressed memories and of the unconscious becoming of urban systems, the dark side of the city, the spaces of confrontation and contamination between organic and inorganic, between nature and artifice. Here, human refuse is metabolized by nature, producing a new horizon of unexplored territories, mutating and virgin, which Stalker has called* Actual Territories.

Perceiving the Becoming. *Perceiving the gap between what is certain, daily, and what is uncertain, to be discovered, generates a sense of disorientation, a state of apprehension which creates a perceptive intensification. All of a sudden space has sense, everywhere there is the possibility of discovery, the fear of an undesired encounter. The gaze becomes more penetrating, the ear is more ready to hear. (From the* Stalker Manifest, http://digilander.libero.it/stalkerlab/tarkowsky/tarko.html*)*

is, in fact, also a concrete action toward modifying it, because the character of the city "isn't determined only by geographic and economic factors, but also by the representation its inhabitants have of it" (IS 94) and "social space is the result of a process of multiple aspects and movements: meaningful and meaningless, perceived and experienced, practiced and theoretical" (Lefebvre 81).

Following in the wake of the first surrealist walkabouts, during which the aim of "drifting aimlessly around the city" was to "put oneself in the condition of verifying subconscious actions, in which the urban center is transformed into an adventurous forest in which stores, street corners, statues reveal their true nature as traps for desire" (Bandini 99). The situationist *drift* proposed transforming entire portions of urban fabric, upsetting times and methods of fruition. As the word suggests, drifting consisted in crossing the city following pathways that were both random and intentional, in which surprise and adventure were combined with precise, cognitive intent. *Getting lost* was part of drifting, just like the condition of disorientation had been for the surrealists: a necessary condition in order to break the topological chains that regulate the use of urban space. They transformed a well-known place, that was crossed every day following fixed and repetitive itineraries, into the equivalent of an unexplored forest, in which the heretofore unperceived spaces, smells, sounds, attractions and repulsions had to be discovered. This act of losing oneself was not blind; it was

Ugo La Pietra, Istruzioni per l'uso della città, *1979.*

rather a conscious act of urban decontextualization, the prelude to a recontextualization that would produce new geographies, measurements of *degrees of freedom*, re-appropriation of existing urban spaces.

Therefore, in this playground

> "getting lost" can result in something other than disorientation. It might pave the way for that state of being "out-of-place" which forces us to reconstruct our reference points, to measure up and redefine ourselves with respect to a different context. In these cases, our re-adaptation lets us "learn and learn" (G. Bateson, 1972), it reactivates an interaction between us and the environment we had taken for granted and which instead – at the risk of that total loss of identity which can happen with each loss – re-emerges, with all its "reasons", its logic, its "feeling". (La Cecla 88)

The urban form that emerges can be that of the two maps Guy Debord made of Paris, in which the city is separated into large islands connected by vectors that indicate passionate attractions, but also that of the labyrinth, which, as Bataille writes, is the topological equivalent of the figure of the player absorbed in his game, a space that exists only as a trajectory, with unidentifiable limits…

But here we are about to enter the next playground, beyond the pure and simple one of the eye: the playground of the body in space…

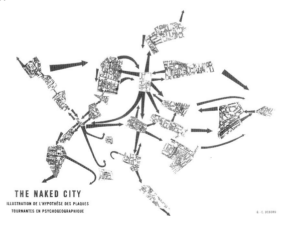

Guy-Ernest Debord, The Naked City, *1957.*

playground 02
The Game of the Body in Space

In 1959, the Situationists, in preparation for the exhibit that would be held at the Stedelijk Museum of Amsterdam the following year, decided to transform rooms 36 and 37 of the museum into a labyrinth whose length could vary "theoretically" from 200 meters to 3 kilometers, depending on the path the visitor followed. The dimensions of the rooms weren't constant, they varied in height and width, some of the passageways were made purposefully difficult and a system of doors that could only open in one direction increased the possibility of getting lost. Forms, dimensions and decorations of the internal space were planned so as to "create a mixed, never-before-seen environment" (IS 94), in which characteristics of the urban environment, like wind, rain and artificial fog, combined with internal elements and other sonorous and visual stimuli. Getting lost became a special event that was experienced through the senses. This labyrinth was the *constructed* equivalent of drifting, in which two separate groups connected by walkie-talkies crossed the city over the space of three days. The same experience of disorientation produced by getting lost in the urban labyrinth was recreated in a space that was completely planned. It was the opportunity to create a "never before seen" space without necessarily having to create the perceptive détournement of elements of the urban context.

Basically, that labyrinth was a form of disorientation which acted on one's instantaneous perceptions rather than on the representation of space. It constituted the passage from an abstract playground – personal and passionate geography, the new constellation

of senses produced by drifting through recognized elements – to a concrete playground, measured, discovered, produced by the immediate relationship between body and the physical, sonorous and visual qualities of a space. In other words, the same passage from a *mediate* to an *immediate* space that was experienced by our patient, "the man who mistook his wife for a hat", when he recognized a glove in the moment in which he tried it on, or rather, in the moment in which that form stopped being a figurative abstraction and became a surface that could be related to a sense – touch – and became an experience that was not mediated by culture.

This is similar to what children experience in the spatial playgrounds, where the dizzying pleasure of playing lies in having an environment in which the body can freely establish new forms of relations – the world as seen from upside down. When reference points and preferential directions disappear, disorientation becomes like the lost feeling of drifting, that interval of freedom in which it is the body that gives meaning to space.

In fact, we can agree with Lefebvre that space "is not pre-existent, empty, endowed with merely formal characteristics […] but is produced by the relationship between body and the material that surrounds it." In fact, "every living body *is* a space and *has* space: it produces itself in it and it produces it. […]. Bodies, the dispersal of energy, produce space and they produce themselves, with their movements, according to the laws of space" (Lefebvre 81).

The form of this playground, the first constructed play architecture we encounter, must then be "never before seen", or in other

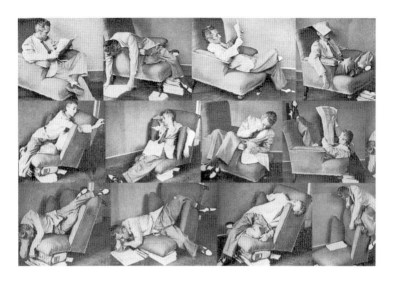

Bruno Munari, Looking for comfort in an uncomfortable armchair, *1950.*

words, it must not communicate its function by means of a codified form; it must, in synthesis, be *informal*, it must overcome the coincidence of form and function and open new space to multiple uses.

In this playground, a table isn't a table and a chair is not a chair, not just because we can barely recognize them, but because we have taken the liberty of dismantling and recomposing them as we please. Or because someone has turned them upside down, since they *don't exist anymore* as recognizable objects, endowed with a precise function. A table *might* be a table, an irregularity in the ground *might* become a seat, just like a dip in the pavement *might* become a place to lie down in, meet in, roll around in, a wall *might* become a diaphragm between two spaces and so on.

Therefore, the functional subdivision of planned space is broken down; this space is traditionally composed of objects with specific *roles* and is abstractly divisible into levels and areas dedicated to different functions. More specifically, the different parts of the body (planes on which one can rest elbows, feet, bottom, etc., planes that delimitate internal and external areas, above and below) and the play ground in certain types of architecture ideally become a continuous plane which is contemporaneously chair, pavement, wall, bed, piazza, façade, etc… in a form which is the

Verner Panton, Living Chair, 1969.

complementary opposite of a labyrinth, with the same capacity to disorient in a space that is continuous rather than discontinuous.

This unrecognizable playground is also unstable, since its inhabitant has to make a choice of creatively finding a space for his activities, where his behavior chooses its own creative relationship with the space by taking it over, and giving the places value of use, creating the conditions by which they become tables, chairs, beds, internal spaces, for resting, for meeting, collective spaces, etc.

But this freedom is two-sided: if the form of the space as a perceptive given can modify our behavior, the opposite can also happen, that the use of one of the spaces is modified by the new relationships which our body establishes with it. For example, in hide-and-seek, when the player discovers and invents spaces for hiding in within the domestic labyrinth: a table becomes a roof, the space between two open doors becomes a room, a closet becomes a place to lie down and curl up in as though it were a recessed bed. And this happens in all those places in the city where different types of behavior take over the spaces – a low wall becomes a seat, the church steps become a living room in which to meet, the open area behind the house hosts infinite soccer games – where, as Sennet writes in his description of a "hot playground", the space, by freeing itself of the form/function relationships, finally

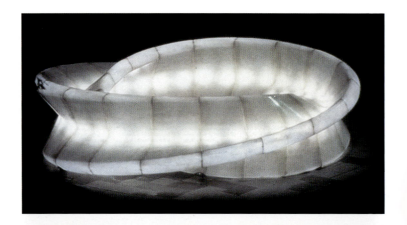

Top: Vito Acconci, Dario Nunez, Luis Vera, Kyle Steinfeld, Peter Dorsey, Möbius bench, *Fukuroi City, Japan 2001*. Bottom: Vito Acconci, Dario Nunez, Peter Dorsey, Sergio Prego, Kyle Steinfeld, Michael Day, Anthony Arnold, Jean Humke, Matthew Wood, Klein-bottle Playground, *2000*.

Vito Acconci, Luis Vera, Celia Imrey, Dario Nunez, Jenny Schrider, Charles Doherty, Saija Singer, Flying floors main ticketing pavillion, *Philadelphia International Airport, USA, 1998.*

Enric Miralles Benedetta Tagliabue, Lungo Mare *chair, produced by Escofet, 2001.*

becomes *narrative*, a place where an experience, a story, an adventure begin:

> A city playground is a place for beginning by escape. […] Kids in an urban playground cut themselves off in play from ties to their home and family; they shun the nice places adults made for them. In these places a conscious fiction is also at work. Kids at the "hot" playground behave as if they were parentless, totally free agents […] as though fiction were fact, that there were no reality before right here, right now. […] The playgrounds that are full all the time in the city are like those at the corner of Sixth Avenue and Third Street, places kids reach by subway as well as on foot. Iron mesh fences frame courts for basketball, with only a few straggly trees. Trucks and honking taxis struggling up Sixth Avenue create a deafening volume of sounds which combines with the portable radios tuned to Latin or rap beats. Everything in this crowded playground is hard surface. Here, though, is a space where time can begin. Linear spaces may be defined as those spaces in which form follows function. Narrative space are, instead, spaces like this playground, places of displacement. […] Time begins to do the work of giving places character when the places are not used as they were meant to be. (Sennet 92)

Alison and Peter Smothson, "street life" in Urban Structuring, 1967.

playground 03
The Game Invades the City

A Spring afternoon in a piazza in a central European city: strolling people distractedly cross the piazza, temporary presences for whom it is nothing more than a quantity of space between the point of departure and the point of arrival; an old lady is feeding the pigeons; and a man is sitting in the shade of a tree, reading a newspaper. There are also some kids, for whom the piazza is something entirely different, they admire its continuity, its changes in height and its slopes; it is like a big playground to skateboard on, that space becomes the elective place of a community for whom nothing else seems to exist, they are happily separated from the dynamics of a city that continues to move around them. (ma0, preliminary notes for *Europan 7*, 2003)

All the space of a city and beyond can be transformed in this playground, where all you need is a minimal contrivance to turn a wide area, the back of a building or a street, into a place where one of these plays can begin:

Changing what is real, events that disturb the "socio-urban and architectonic myths and rites," all aim to create a temporary crisis in the structure of use and fruition of the city and its architecture, altering its responses to those of the expectations of its users, interrupting the system of anticipation of the user, who is blocked by stereotyped rules. (Orlandoni, Vallino 77)

Haus-Rucker-co, Giant Billiard, *1970, Museum des 20. Jahrunderts, Vienna, from* AD, *April 1970.*

Stalker, *Transborderline/Globall Game*, 2000

*For three exhibits (*La ville le jardin la memoire *at Villa Medici in Rome, the VII Biennale d'Architettura of Venice,* Manifesta 3 *in Lubjana) Stalker created* Transborderline, *an ideal structure for crossing borders, taking across the borders the stories and the desires of the Kurdish refugees, the immigrants and the nomads who live at Campo Boario, the ex-Mattatoio in Rome, where the group has recently been working.* Globall Game *is the apparatus in which the stories are collected, it is able to cross barriers and differences, generating a collective condition of "extraneous" play, in which everyone is an actor, a player. The game takes the ball well beyond the* Actual Territory *of Campo Boario, across the canals and fields of Venice, involving other "strangers", until it symbolically stops at the border between Italy and Slovenia, where many illegal immigrants enter Italy.*

Top to bottom: Campo Boario, Venice, Lubjana, the Italian-Slovenian border.

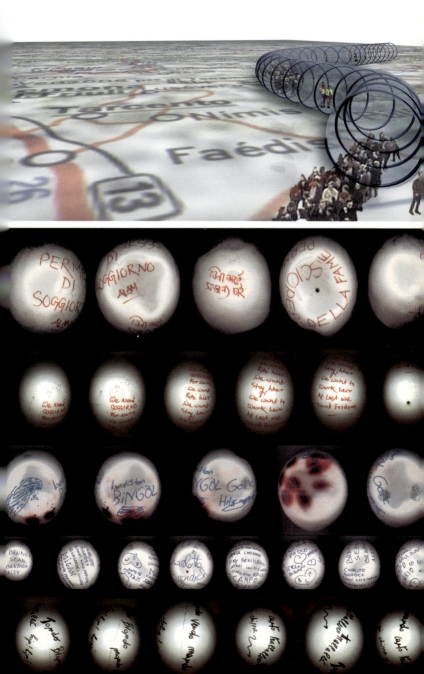

In fact, collective space is, as opposed to private space, a place where the individual falsely believes he is the *dominus* of the surrounding objects, creating a universe in his own image which is rigidly structured according to typologies that clearly indicate the range of activities that are permitted within it. He can block or explicitly prohibit every other activity by means of architectonic strategies (for example: seats that can't be used for sleeping on, fences that close off areas dedicated to playing, walls that keep people from walking across green areas, etc.) and relevant signs (*ball playing is forbidden...*) which, added up, bear spatial witness to all the prohibitions that are tacitly shared within the collective group.

This space in particular shows its *rigidity* and *fixedness* with respect to a usage that could change continuously with passing time, and following the wishes of its inhabitants, and it helps produce what Raoul Vaneighem called *conditioning* in his "Treatise on Etiquette for the Young Generations", which was a great success with young people during the protest years that straddled the 1960's and 1970's. This conditioning required a *reversal of perspective*:

> Conditioning has the function of placing and moving every person along a hierarchical scale. The reversal of perspective implies a sort of anti-conditioning, not a new type of conditioning, but a playing tactic: reconversion (détournement). The reversal of perspective substitutes knowledge with praxis, experience with freedom, mediation with the desire for immediacy. It sanctions the triumph of a group of human relations founded on three inseparable poles: participation, communication, realization. The reversal of perspective means ceasing to see with the eyes of the community, of ideology, family, others. It means solidly taking possession of oneself, choosing oneself as the point of departure and as the center. (Veneigem 99)

Urban games, which not by chance became a strategy of some architects to occupy public space during those years when people fought for "imagination in power", became happenings in which spatial strategies that were instantaneous, ephemeral, lightweight, often inflatable, intervened dynamically between body and space. Or better, they intervened between bodies and space, extending the disorienting power of contact games to the community, involving individuals – who were sometimes there by chance, surprised by an unexpected event – in trajectories, physical contact, power fields that absorbed them in a public space, where hierarchies and roles were annihilated. They all became *players* in an alienated context which broke the ties between the form of public space and pre-ordained behavior.

Not just that: since – often, but not always – mobile constructed spaces, which modify themselves as the game proceeds, involve the player in *movement* from the urban context, transforming the passive user into *actors* who can participate in the creation of ways and times to use urban spaces.

> The alternative, the answer to psycho-physical automatisms, to reified behavior, can only be the re-discovery of behavior that is an end to itself and a proposal of creative behavior. If self-knowledge, individual liberation, the definitive removal of anxiety is the privileged goal, and alternative behavior is the precise state of this achievement, then architecture will simply be the instrument of behavioral induction. (Orlandoni, Vallino 77, pp. 105-106)

But urban games hardly every work autonomously within public space, on the contrary, they sometimes become spatial support

Ant Farm, Inflatable, 1971, Ant Farm Archives, *courtesy of Chip Lord.*

Santiago Cirugeda, Strategies for subversive occupation / Recuperate the street, *2000.* http://idensitat.cccb.org/particip/cirugeda/estrategias_e.htm.

City Mine(d), Bal. http://www.citymined.org/

Martin Ruiz de Azùa, Casa Basica, *1999.*

MaO: A square in Bari, a "Sitting Around" Bench, a Preliminary Project from 2001

A public space that can be continuously reconfigured according to the wishes of its inhabitants: the seating is entirely composed of rotating benches that can be moved into the shade of the trees on hot days, or on the contrary, they can be moved into the sunshine on colder days. They can be moved under the light of the lamp-posts to facilitate reading at night, or they can be placed in the shadows for some privacy…

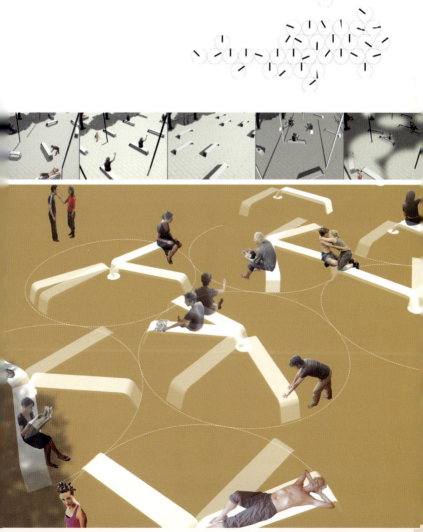

instruments in a wider game, which involves disciplines that flank architecture in the *participatory* planning of constructed areas where architecture dissolves into projects of communication, of construction of relationships. Space, constructed space, thus becomes the product of a process in which the architect is one of the agents, we could even say one of the actors, who participates in the great game of constructing the city.

We are at a crossroads: on the one hand a type of architecture that reacquires its social role as an alienating disposition stimulating new behavior, producing new relationships between individuals and space, between individuals and the community; and on the other, a complementary practice that produces architecture, but starting with the complex and participatory game of actors in the field. The first tries to use its own instruments to measure its capacity to have a bearing on the way space is used, the second considers space as the product – as Archigram wrote, "a ghostly reminder" – of the creative, complex and definitely *political* process of collective behavior.

The decision to follow the first path becomes at this point a necessity, if one doesn't want to get lost in an intricate web of stories and experiences which could never find their due space in these pages, but it is also a conscious choice to continue understanding how the form of a space interacts with the uncertain and unpredictable play of our existence.

Just around the corner, however, an even more complex playground is waiting for us, the entire city.

Alison and Peter Smithson, Golden Lane: street deck, *1952-53.*

playground 04
The Play City

Provide every streetlamp with on-off switches, for an illumination that is at the public's disposal. ("Projet d'embellisement de la ville de Paris", in *Potlatch*, n. 23)

This is the most difficult playground to create, not just because of its complexity. We are faced with such an increase in scale that it presupposes the existence of an entire society willing to play in it, or even, like the Situationists in the wake of Huizinga, imagine a new species of human beings, the *homo ludens*, who supposedly freed himself from work with the help of the new technology of automation, and supposedly dedicated himself entirely to the creative construction of collective spaces.

The game lies in searching for happiness in the natural and innate desire to decide one's own life, constantly moving around in search of contexts and climates that are more favorable to one's personal mood, or more realistically, in search of employment possibilities, becoming *nomads* in search of new opportunities for discovery and adventure, living in Constant's *New Babylon* freed from work, or enjoying the freedom of choice offered to us by the society of consumption, like one of the many figures that crowd the instant cities of Archigram.

The game lies in the opportunities that collective life offers, in the unpredictable and fascinating relationships that can spring from meeting others, in an urban space where one doesn't have to build high walls to protect one's home. On the contrary, these walls can be reduced to a thin membrane, a minimal protection from atmospheric agents, open to exchange and confrontation. Here, identity becomes a choice and no longer a refuge, sometimes one of the elements to put into play – or perhaps only one of the masks to choose from among the various *lifestyles* which the market offers. One drifts on the surface of the planet without fear, mixing in with different cultures, appreciating and respecting different wisdoms and customs.

This game can perhaps be only imagined, if we don't search, with a healthy dose of optimism, for a homo sapiens inside each member of our society who aspires to become a *homo ludens*. The playground is a city that knows how to interact with the nat-

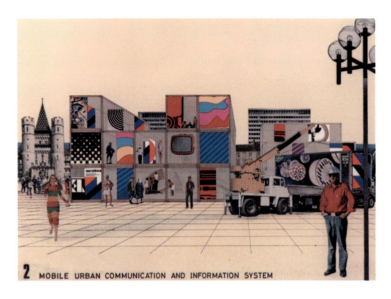

Werner Blasel, Ernest Persche, Lucius Burckhardt, Mobile urban communication and information system, ADI/Casabella *competition* The City as a Significant Environment, *1973.*

ural mobility of the human being, it can contaminate the permanence of architecture with the impermanence of lived life, it can transform the need for shelter into the opportunity for encounters. At the same time, it is the answer to the more or less expressed needs and stimuli for a liberation from choices that are impossible with the present form of urban spaces.

The simplest way to achieve this could be to extend certain characteristics of the preceding playgrounds to the urban scale, constructing indefinite, not-yet-codified spaces for various and spontaneous uses, in a phenomenon of re-appropriation on the part of the inhabitants/players.

Spaces that can be searched for in the history of architecture, starting where the criticism of the coincidence of form and function is strongest, starting with the proposals of a group of "heretics" of functionalist orthodoxy: Team X.

In 1953, at the ninth CIAM convention, Alison and Peter Smithson presented the concept of *streets-in-the-air* "as a possible

Constant, Eastern Sector, New Babylon, *1959*.

replacement for the basic principles the organization had established twenty years earlier in its infamous document, the Athens Charter. They argued that the appropriate pattern of associations between people and functions cannot be predicted. Social groupings are the product of "looseness" of spatial organization and easy communication rather than fixed patterns. Architects should provide a structure that is open to unexpected and changing relationships" (Wigley 98). In the same way, Aldo Van Eyck, with whom Constant collaborated in the creation of some of his playgrounds, – and not by chance! – in 1955 created in his Amsterdam orphanage a "labyrinth form with endless, different pathways, and a network of micro-climates generated by the user rather than by the architect" (*ibid.*), which later expanded until it ideally covered the entire surface of the planet in Constant Niewenhuis' *New Babylon*, where the city becomes a labyrinth which multiplies the chances for encounters and collective creations.

From that moment on, until the reaction of the early 70's, architects throughout the world began to produce urban visions which profoundly questioned the axioms of the functionalist city. Architecture constructed around the changing and mobile character of its inhabitants and events of the collective city was "considered a departure datum for the Smithsons, to incorporate within

Aldo Van Eyck, Dijkstraat playground, Amsterdam 1954. Orphanage, Amsterdam 1955.

the new buildings, which would respect the reign of the 'passing presence' and 'chance encounter'" (Curtis 99). They were reduced in the Archigram montages into a pure emanation of a collective state of mind, in which architecture – geometry, stylistic features, language, etc. – first became the background, the scenery of a story – a *play* – in which the leading character is for the first time the human figure.

So, years after the Smithsons, that *looseness* that was idealized to free the individual from the spatial bonds of architecture, was enlarged until it became the continuous and undifferentiated plane of the Archizoom *No-stop City*, an immense supermarket city in which to freely settle down, the paradoxical annihilation of form through the radical adhesion to an indeterminate function, in which another powerful instrument for the creation of this playground appears, technology:

> You can be wherever you want, bring your tribe or your family with you. There is no need for shelter, thanks to the particular climatic conditions and thanks to the modifications that have been made to the thermal-regulatory mechanisms to guarantee the maximum comfort. If you want, you can have fun building a shelter, or making a house, or playing architect. All you have to do is insert a plug: the desired microclimate will immediately be at your disposal (temperature, humidity…); put the plug in and you will be connected to the information network, push a button and you will have water and food. (Prestinenza Puglisi 1999)

Archizoom, No-stop City, *1970.*

Complementary to the indefiniteness of architectonic space, technology can therefore become one of the instruments to help architecture evolve from a simple refuge into a machine capable of molding itself based on the desires and necessities of the moment: "The architectonic complex will be modifiable. Its aspect will change in part or entirely according to the desires of its inhabitants" (IS 94).

In a particularly *technophile* period, when the constructive process of the 1960's seemed able to produce *science-fiction* scenarios, many architects imagined cities that were built from modular, transportable units, sometimes as light as a dress, as Ionel Schein proposes: "The forms will have the character of wrappers, of portable shelters" (M.-A. Brayer) sometimes becoming true double skins, inflatable, sensual, light-weight, ready to use; or composed of mobile modules to be hooked onto stationary infrastructures, like Yona Friedman's project for a spatial city: "architecture that permits the necessary continuous transformations in order to ensure 'social mobility', thanks to the environments and urbanistic structures that can be assembled and reassembled according to the intentions of its inhabitants" where "mobility is certainly that of a new liberty given to the user" and "the regular pattern of the spatial city is a 'white page' on which the user writes down, in a constantly unpredictable way, his own space, he draws his own habitat" (*ibid.*).

In substance, using the words of Archigram, this playground can be constructed generating a "much more permissive situation

This page: IaN+, project for the DADA office building competition in Florence, 2001. Left: concept; below: longitudinal section, functional diagram, view of a 3d model, external view. Facing page: Foreign Office Architects, Port Terminal Yokohama, 1995-2002. Top: possible uses (theater, sports), general views of the construction, the pit for open-air performances.

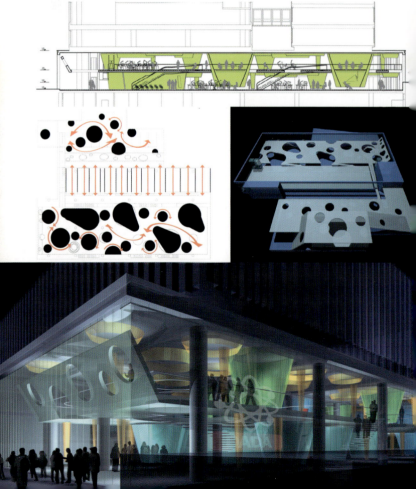

Playground 04: the Play City

The looseness of the play city: two examples of contemporary architecture in which the degree of indefiniteness of space allows the architecture to adapt itself to multiple uses, to fluid spatial relationships. In the Ian+ project "the main space of the DADA offices is a new open space, in which the usual two-dimensional dividing elements placed between the different work areas are substituted by three-dimensional units which both separate and unite, influencing adjacent areas with their presence", clear separations between the different work zones disappear. At the Yokohama Terminal by FOA, the ambiguous form of the urban space is at the same time park, building, and exchange point, it encourages multiple uses, creative interpretation of space, encounters.

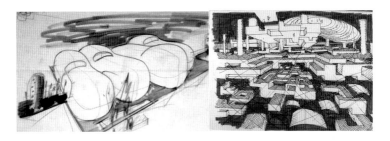

Ionel Schein, Project for a mobile library, *1957. Yona Friedman,* La ville spatiale, *1958-1960.*

where people will just assemble the bits and pieces that they collect together" (Curtis 99) and where "the determination of your environment need no longer be left in the hands of the designer of the building: it can be turned over to you yourself. You turn the switches and choose the conditions to sustain you at that point in time. The 'building' is reduced to the role of a carcass – or less" (Archigram 91). Just look at the project for Cedric Price's *Fun Palace* in which "all horizontal elements – services, roofs, floors – all walling elements, environmental equipment, escalators, etc. were to be impermanent, mobile, and interchangeable" (Banham 76).

If we therefore want to give people back "their right to elaborate their own habitat in private or in a group, to participate in the creation of their own context" (Toraldo di Francia 2001) then the architecture of the city of play has to become *interactive* right down to the smallest details, from a spatial point of view to perceptive and sensorial points of view. The citizen of New Babylon can, for example, choose from "a vast gamma of dividing walls, materials, different textures and colors, that are also different in their thermo-acoustical qualities" (Constant 74) and "can, in any moment, wherever he is, change the area, regulating the volume of the sounds, the intensity of the light, the olfactory environment, the temperature" (*ibid.*).

But in this technological drift toward the mobile and formless architecture that the Coop Himmelblau compared to clouds, "symbols in a state of rapid change" that "form and transform themselves depending on the complex interplay of different situations" (Coop Himmelblau 66) we come up against the very limit of solid material in architecture, the massive transformations of production methods of urban space, which certainly don't depend on the will of the architect. We are therefore obliged to reduce the *fluidity* and the *interactivity* of architectonic space into *flexibility*, with which important buildings like Piano and Roger's Centre Pompidou have been built, pale heirs of a play architecture that didn't wait for the evolution of the human species and technology in order to become a building.

This paradox is a bit like playing soccer with a stone, architecture can free itself by choosing extremely simple technologies of adaptation, or, on the contrary, by becoming a *sensitive interface*, molding itself according to the desires of its inhabitants through the emission and the reception of sensorial stimuli sounds, smells, lights.

> Given the participation of a large number of people in the emission and the reception of images and sounds, perfected telecommunication becomes an important auxiliary in social play behavior. Like the painter creates an infinite variety of forms, contrasts and styles from a few colors, thus the Neo-Babylonians can ceaselessly vary their environment, renewing it, recreating it. (Constant 74)

The physical and material limits of space become indistinct, extending themselves into a "multitude of spaces" (Serres 72) that are immaterial and synthetic, generated by the new technology of

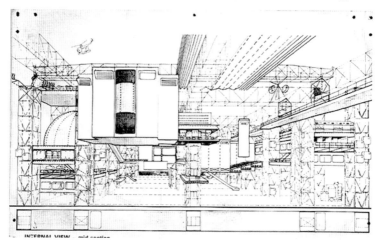

Cedric Price, Fun Palace, *1961.*

PLAYGROUND 04. THE PLAY CITY: BETWEEN CHOICE AND SELF-CONSTRUCTION

Two projects proposing different solutions to the spontaneous configuration of one's habitat, made possible in the M'house by the combination of basic functional elements and differentiated wall panels, and in Living Carpet by the open space on the roof that can be put to different uses, including the construction of another room, which – like the tesserae of a mosaic – contributes to the definition of public space in continuous change.

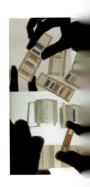

This page: ACTAR Arquitectura, M'house, "á la carte" houses; concept, plastic, perspective. Facing page: ma0, Living Carpet, Europan 6 competition, Porto, Portugal; concept, perspective views, perspective section.

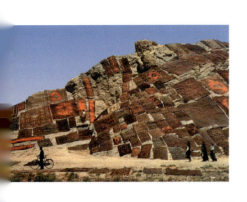
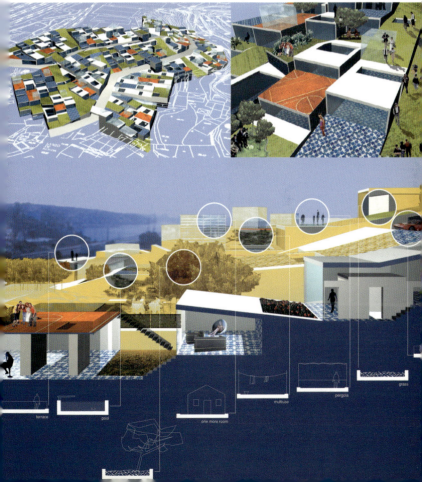

communication, and the city of play opens into a new playground which, like the first, is totally immaterial but entirely technological, chemical and electronic.

playground 05
The Game of Instant Architecture

The fifth playground is a place where the solidity of space and the volatility of electrons meet. It is that uncertain region where two worlds overlap in the search for a relationship between *media* that are substantially different, but into which both enter as part of that "multiplicity of spaces" we live in. One world is made of matter, it helps establish the contacts between people in the reality of a physical environment. It is also the instrument for creating concrete needs like finding shelter, sleeping and meeting. The other world is immaterial, volatile, it instantly propagates itself by means of devices, interfaces that are limited, localized, but that can also let us enter spaces much vaster than a cathedral, the spaces of technological imagination.

The result of this meeting of the worlds is a sort of instant architecture, in which the perceived and communicative data cannot be separated from the spatial data, in which the presence of a receptor/emitter – man – instantly changes the context, in a configuration which can never be repeated. It is the interactivity, that phenomenon which is in the nature of every living organism, by which every action corresponds, through an ecosystem, to a *feedback* which isn't always the same, which is basically different from the linear concept of *reaction*, transported onto the living body of architecture.

This grafting is as powerful as it is sometimes incongruent, always balanced between choice and control, between turning on a light bulb and creating space.

If the main objective of play architecture is that of reconciling the individual with his environment, overcoming that form of spatial alienation which is caused by the impossibility of transforming it according to one's desires, operating creatively within the "zone of uncertainty between subjectivity and objectivity, between the imagined and reality" (Morin 74), then technology can become a very powerful instrument of modulation.

Once again, we will start with a space designed by the Situationists, in the *Cavern of Antimatter* which Pinot Gallizio created in the René Drouin gallery in Paris in 1959:

> In this room of informal painting, which was also supposed to have smells (with resinous, herb-based perfumes) and sounds (with the presence of the "tereminofono" behind the walls) the energy which was to involve the spectator was supposed to be created by a continuous and circular exchange of biochemical, biological and psychic processes. (Bandini 1999)

In an infinitely less complex context from a technological point of view of the many interactive spaces today – whose most feasible device is the "tereminofono", an instrument used by musicians to produce modulations in sound, thanks to its "sensitivity" to bodily presences – the Situationists created a total architecture, even if, as Debord notes, it is still only scenery, and moreover, within the delimited and separated spaces of a gallery. *New Babylon* would extend that totality to the entire urban space.

In this playground, architecture's field of action is extended to the sensorial world that has been reduced by the norms of the rational city to a question of environmental hygiene, mixing with chemistry, electronics, and creating a never-before-seen hybrid of space, technology and state of mind.

> We find ourselves, therefore, faced with an aptitude for planning that is aimed at organizing certain conditions of environmental comfort. Sound, light, energy, etc. come under the direct programming of the planner, the architect; or better, technology-architecture becomes the external nervous system of man. (Orlandoni, Vallino 77)

At a certain point, then, the radical experiences of the 1960's seem to find a formula to evaporate the repressive forms that were resistant to real space in artificially created, lysergic worlds. For example, "with Haus-Rucker, we assist at the construction of artificial environments, *Caschi*, in which a quantity of sensorial, visual, and olfactory stimuli are introduced which tend to expand the field of perceptive possibilities and to create sensations similar to those induced by hallucinogens"(*ibid.*).

PLAYGROUND 05. THE CITY OF INSTANT ARCHITECTURE

In this research of interactivity, architecture tries to free itself from physical and material constraints to become as mobile and lightweight as a fluid, mixing itself with the liquidity of electronic images, or transforming itself, thanks to complex and expensive technology, into amazing interactive installations, like Aegis *or the* H2O Pavilion.

This page: Marco Pastore, Valentina Sabatelli and Nilufer Kozikoglu: LEISURATORtm. An adaptable eco-mechanical landscape for games and urban sports, the result of a project research on "responsive environments" that was begun in October 2001 at the Architectural Association. awg_AllesWirdGut: turnOn experimental housing vision 2000-2002. The house is reduced to a series of modules that can be freely connected; the use of space is optimized by doing away with the distinction between floors, walls and ceiling. Concept, prototype in action, view of a module, prototype on exhibit at the Vitra Design Museum, Germany, Weil am Rhein. Next page: dECOi, Aegis Hyposurface, *1998-2000; Lars Spuybroek-Nox,* H2O Pavilion, *Neeltjie Jans, Netherlands.*

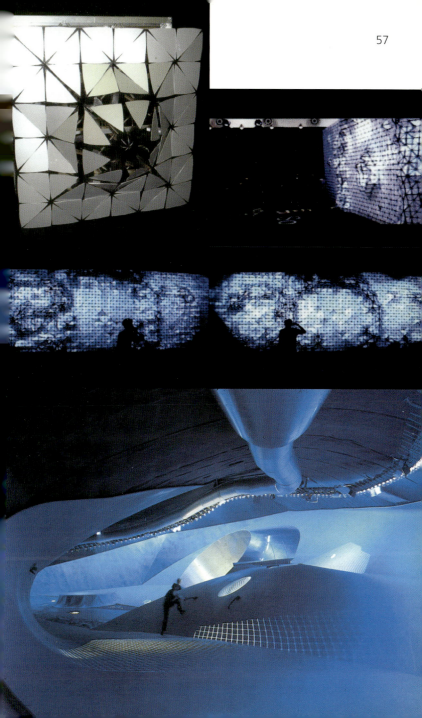

The work of the early Coop Himmelblau "aims at exploring – we are close to body art – the communicative possibilities of the body. This is viewed as an emitter of signals, like a system of fluids that architecture captures and makes perceptive. For the Viennese group, architecture must be the extension of human sensibility, a technological system which, by overlaying the body, clarifies its existence" (*ibid.*).

This path leads progressively to "architecture that is imaginary, immaterial. Friedrich St. Florian experimented with rooms created by light and laser beams, Hans Hollein exhibited 'non-physical' environments: the extension of the universe was a television position, a 'pulverization of environments' created spaces made of perfume and the 'architectonic pill' had the power to simulate nonexistent rooms" (Feuerstein 2001).

The possibility of transforming space was therefore resolved by a liberating prospective of psychedelic transformation called *Enviropill – sit and dream it all* (Curtis 99).

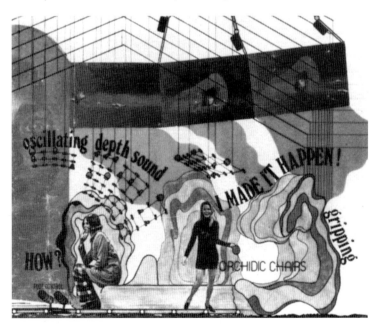

Archigram, Instant City, Environmental jukebox interior, *from AD, May 1969.*

Haus-Rucker-co, Mind Expander, 1968-69.

But at the same time, architecture's field of action was expanding beyond the *here* and *now* of local space, toward an imaginary and communicative territory which began to branch out globally.

Another, more long-lasting consequence of this grafting of technology onto the body of architecture is, in fact, the possibility of transforming a room into an interactive, media device, in which interpersonal, communication space flows into that of telecommunications, in a spatial experience that is integrated, collective and urban.

"Today, the new architecture is made of information. Architecture is only one of the many means of communication: telephone, radio, satellites, etc, are the other means" (Orlandoni, Vallino 77). As Marie-Ange Brayer wrote concerning Archigram's vision of instant cities, "this ephemeral architecture is the 'software' of a 'hardware' that is the inert, static, reified city."

But these experiences in those years didn't go beyond proposing "involvement spaces" in which "the visual elements of the city would represent themselves, put themselves on show, ask for the approval of their vast communicative potential, their presumed lucidity. This approval is obtained by involvement, activism and vitality imposed by the redundancy of information, signs that act on a subliminal level" where "the involvement is nothing more than uncritical participation; the called-for freedom is only a freedom from standard behavior, a choice of consumption" (Orlandoni, Vallino 77).

The game ends at the end of the 1960's in the freedom of choice between the images that society produced as pure representations of lifestyles. It picks up again, with very different potential, during the years of potentially *equal* and *horizontal* communication offered by the network. This launched a line of research into the creative capacity of architecture as interface which is still going on today, on the crest of an unyielding tension between material and immaterial spaces, between a "nearness" that resists with the weight and gravity that are natural to constructed figures and a "distance" that continuously expands, but which enters every day into the intimate spaces of life, opening windows onto new, boundless playgrounds.

> O still-powerful lords of the earth, sooner or later you will give us machines for playing [...]. We will stare as we please at the images of the movie cameras, televisions, which the collective genius of the people has created and which you have poorly used to imprison us in the absolute kingdom of boredom. (Pinot Gallizio, "Discorso sulla pittura industriale e su un'arte unitaria applicabile", in IS 94)

Archigram, Instant City visits Santa Monica, *from* AD, *May 1969.*

PLAYGROUND 06. RELATIONSHIP DEVICES

ma0: PLAY the world of videogames, *Palazzo delle Esposizioni, Rome 2002.* *This project researches the limit between digital and real space: a continuous screen for back projections folds itself along projective beams, generating a continuous and three-dimensional imaginary landscape.*

playground 06
Invaders of Space

"This is 'The Construct', it's our loading program. We can load anything, from clothing to equipments, weapons, training simulations, anything we need."
"Right now we're inside a computer program?"
"Is it really so hard to believe? [...]
"This... this isn't real?"
"What is real? How do you define real? If you're talking about what you can fell, what you can smell, what you can taste and see then 'real' is simply electrical signals interpreted by your brain..."

Night Driver, *Atari, 1976*.

In 1971, in the full flowering of the "radical" phenomenon of Italian and international architecture, something new happened. The architects certainly didn't notice, but it was the beginning of a path that would lead to the creation of one of the most vast and powerful collective playgrounds humanity has ever created. Atari produced *Computer Space*, the first commercial videogame in history. It was only the slightly more evolved version of the very first videogame, Spacewar, which the MIT laboratories had created for fun a decade earlier. The intervening years seemed to have served to miniaturize the machine from the size of a closet to that of a phone booth, the so-called coin-operated machine which would slowly start to make a noisy and often crowded corner for itself in bars throughout the world. It is the same technology that architects had enthusiastically integrated into their projections, without actually going beyond a spectacular form of a multimedia amusement park or psychedelic, audiovisual stimulations. In those years, it started becoming electronic, taking its first steps and drafting inventions which over the space of a couple of decades, at first very slowly and then increasingly rapidly, would radically change the way we communicate. Arpanet, for example, a Pentagon project to connect various computers scattered throughout the United States, the embryo of what would later become Internet (D'Alessandro 2002).

Like every other story dealing with technological evolution, we don't know where this one will take us, and if we still find it hard to understand what we need a 20 gigahertz processor for – which a rough calculation using Moore's law puts on the market in about ten years – we can forget imagining the convergence between public and private communications instruments, increasingly powerful computers and games...

The fact is that history always seems to follow a different path from what we had imagined in science fiction books. Instead of taking us to Mars to meet our cousins from the solar system, it is transforming us into a sort of new collective organism, which is constantly connected by a tightly-woven network of portable and non-portable devices for the purpose of exchanging information, sensations, and new forms of consumer items.

Nevertheless, we have to try. Like Pinot Gallizio, who prefigured a future which did come true, even if it was neutralized within the range of consumption and leisure. It's always that way:

the visions of the future always seem to come true with a minus sign in front of them; today, at the cost of one or two average-size salaries, it can be found on the shelves of electronics stores. And try mixing together different ingredients, preparing a culture to grow visions in that have yet to come true, lean forward and at the same time lean back to understand the nature of a space that is still doubtlessly immature, but which already today contains the premises for creating a playground that has never been seen before.

What happened during the 1960's when the MIT researchers were programming *Spacewar* was the irruption into the world of games of a space that was completely different, despite the simplicity of its rules, the abstraction of space it represented, and the scarce opportunity it offered for creatively and strategically interpreting the rules and the playing field. *Spacewar*, like the games that were soon to follow, became a commercial phenomenon of such proportions that it turned into the driving force of technological evolution for commercial computer applications – just think about the dizzying succession of increasingly powerful video boards that are created more for the players of T*omb Raider* than for professional rendering and animation applications – they intro-

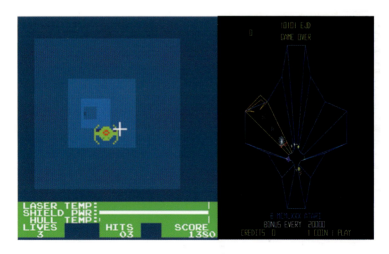

This page: Tunnel Hunt, *1981, Atari. Tempest, 1980, Atari*

duced a component of magic into the game that has marked the beginning of all visual arts:

> In order to understand this magic, one must return to the "double" theme that had already emerged while talking about death. The existence of a double is proven by the mobile shadow that accompanies everyone, by the split personality that occurs in dreams, and by the double that is reflected in water, that is, the image. As a consequence, the image isn't a simple image, it carries within itself the presence of the double of the represented being and it permits one, through this intermediary, to act upon this being. This is the action that is truly magic: a rite of evocation through the image, a rite of invocation to the image, a rite of possession of the image (the spell). (Morin 74)

It might appear reckless to talk about *doubles* with reference to the first videogames, in which the player had to identify with a small triangle outlined in white – the spaceship – on a black background dotted with intermittent white dots – outer space – or with a small, moving white line – the pong racket. But Morin's words about the first graffiti that man drew thousands of years ago somehow explain the gap between the first videogames, with

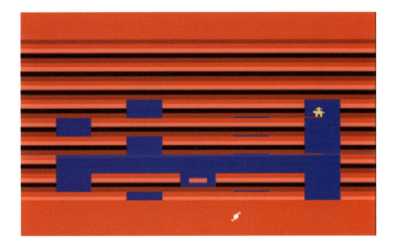

Tutankham, *1982, Konami.*

all their limits, and all the other games to come: the playing space is a totally visual space, dynamic *in-lusio* within which, for the first time, we can let our double interact.

And yet the artificial context we enter the moment we put our coin into the coin-op or the moment we turn our console on was – and still is – an infinitely less complex context than that of a game of chess, or of a hiding place, not to mention of life, which that game proposes to mirror. It is a system of constrictive rules, a rigidly pre-arranged request, and it is completely *private*, like a game of solitaire.

But the machines that ran the first games couldn't guarantee this complexity: they had few k's of memory and only monochromatic screens to achieve a goal that at the time was apparently unreachable: to *simulate* real space through graphic and technological construction devices, to represent space on the flat surface of the screen, with an extremely creative and economic use of resources.

"Programmers did the best they could, balancing the aesthetic needs with considerations of game play and frequently overwhelming technical constraints. Often the aesthetics came last" (Noah Falstein, *Portrait of the Artists in a Young Industry*, *http://www.theinspiracy.com/ArPAYSIG.htm*).

The history of the first thirty years of this playground is the continuous search for a greater similarity between the spatial and perceptive qualities of the scene beyond the screen and those of reality, sometimes to the detriment of the complexity of the *gameplay*, using the limited resources of the programmers to overcome the original sin of videogames, the fact that they are nothing more than an image.

The game space was therefore transformed from the two-dimensional plane of the very early years to three-dimensional space. It was the invention of *Night Driver*, where the marvel lies in watching two lines of white squares move toward the observer, getting larger and larger as they approach, simulating the reflectors on the edges of a road at night. It was perhaps one of the most extraordinary cases of graphic economy in videogames, but its effect was overwhelming for the prospects it opened up, and which would soon establish a few typologies of game space, like the labyrinth.

With its excellent ratio of spectacular to power of calculus (in fact, it hides spaces beyond its walls, so that the machine can elaborate them in portions – which are called levels in gameplay and which represent more than just the winning succession of playing fields), but also with its narrative capacity, the labyrinth rapidly becomes one of the most wide-spread spaces. It is the strategy of the complicated for the complex, but it is also a space that forces the player to constantly orient himself, making the space full of surprises, opportunities, dangers.

But what is just as important as three-dimensionality in the playing field is its quality as matter and the enormous potential of vectors is soon abandoned as too abstract, geometric and synthetic with respect to a means that inexorably points to the construction of credible spaces.

Research concentrates on the definition of the surface of the objects, through the construction of patterns which, using pixels like the tesserae of a mosaic, give videogames the chromatic and tactile qualities – rough, smooth or sparkling – of real space, simulating grass in a meadow, or a brick wall, or the definition of unusual forms of architecture, like in *Savage Bees* or *Rockman*, or again, like in *Street Fighter II*, the definition of highly detailed backgrounds that in no way interact with the dynamics of the game, if not for the fact that they create more atmospheric and realistic scenery than previous games had. And when the calculating power permits, the pattern is abandoned and substituted by *texture*.

The surfaces of the materials are no longer defined by graphic approximations of real surfaces, but rather, a photographic image of real or invented matter is applied onto the faces of the polygons that define the three-dimensional elements of the game (the vector returns covered in matter). The result is completely realistic from a distance, but crumbles unrealistically as we approach, like in *Doom*, where we hit a wall: the insurmountability of that limit is shown in its entirety, denouncing the limits of hardware and software in mimicking reality. The space we are immersed in crumbles, it becomes illegible.

The fact is that this race toward verisimilitude between videogame space and reality – be it pure invention or based on facts that really happened or on real places – seems to tend toward a vanishing point that is rapidly approaching. The calculating power and graphic capacities of pc's or the new consoles will, sooner or later, fulfill this desire for a double identity, and perhaps they will finally let videogames roam within spaces and stories whose potentialities are still unknown, far from the cages of verisimilitude – as can already be seen in Rez, the first psychedelic videogame of the new generation, a contemporary version of the vector hallucinations of Tempest.

But parallel to this race for verisimilitude – which calls to mind the first moving images of cinema, with the terrified spectators fleeing from the sight of a train racing toward the movie camera, as though it could cross the screen and mow down the entire audience – this network connecting the first, privileged nodes of Arpanet progressively extended at an exponential rate until it entered into the private space of millions of people, generating Internet as we know it today – and who knows what it will be like tomorrow – and opening the limits of this playground to a multitude of players, who could finally leave the private dimension of the screen, which until then had been a sort "narcissistic mirror for the single computer user" (Zimmerman 99) on which games of

Nova 2001, 1983 UPL

solitaire were played, rarely diluted by multiplayer features.

In this way, entire communities have sprung up over the past years, groups that meet and play on some asteroid in a faraway galaxy, or within the folds of virtual cities, hosted by some server who knows where.

Games like *Ultima Online* manage to create parallel worlds inhabited by tens of thousands of *avatars*, digital doubles created by the players which play out an infinity of roles, from the more obvious ones of warriors with special powers and characteristics that are accumulated over hours and hours of playtime, to "normal" copies of individuals who interact in cities that are just like ours, like the *Sims Online*, a contemporary version of the historic *Sim City*, in which the game consists in living a fairly banal life, made up of single-story houses and fiancés who need to be kept happy. Statistically, the players in these worlds are not just adolescents, but an increasing number of *adults* creating *clans* which confront each other in international challenges – or galactic ones, if you will – beginning relationships, falling in love, getting married,

ASO - Armored Scrum Object , 1985 SNK; Ark Area, 1988 UPL.

depending on the type of game: role-playing, strategic, shoot-em-up, hentai, etc.

Basically, videogame space turns from private to *public*, to such an extent that it mixes life on this side of the screen with the simulated one: in a study of Ultima Online it was found that a percentage of the romantic relationships that were created while playing the game were transformed into true love stories with very predictable consequences…

But not only that: the complexity of the system produces such possibilities for the exchange of information between the players that they have started sharing strategies to resolve some of the more difficult steps, to the point of producing actual *proposals for changing the rules*. The same thing happens with hackers, or in *open source* scientific communities which, through the free contributions of single programmers scattered throughout the world, have produced Linux, an operative system for computers and servers that is in continuous – effective – improvement, in a constant and open exchange of knowledge.

> There is a lot of congruence between gamers and Open Source coders – with the former applying their talents to the entertainers experiences rather than server protocols or operating systems. (J.C. Herz, *Gaming and the Art of Innovation, Doors of Perception 7: Flow*, http://flow.doorsofperception.com/content/herz_trans.html)

> As Pekka Himanen relates in his study of hacker ethics, working with and sharing of code is seen as joyous play. Himanen quotes hacker Eric Raymond expounding the mantra, You need to care. You need to play. You need to be willing to explore. (Graeme Murrell, *A Drifters Guide to Physical and Virtual Urban Space, Monocular Texts*, http://www.monoculartimes.co.uk/texts/architexts/driftersguide1.shtml)

J.C. Herz, author of *Joystick Nation*, tells how the possibility of creating personalized objects in the *Sims* soon resulted in 90% of the game space being occupied by products belonging to the population of players, who not only defined new contexts for the game but also stimulated new and unexpected behavior:

> The Sims objects are not self-contained executable programs. And they are not static data either. They function in prescribed ways, interact

semi-autonomously, and exhibit behaviours within a dynamic framework. New objects contain behaviours that reconfigure the local environment. The Sims don't know how to play soccer for instance. But if a soccer ball – a software object, containing all the rules for playing soccer – is dropped into their midst, they will form teams and start playing soccer. Player-created plug-ins and mods intersect with game engines in a similar fashion. (J.C. Herz, *op. cit.*)

But the possibilities in the hands of the players seem to go well beyond the creation of objects that populate and interact with their environments according to unpredictable behavior. Players create game variations – mods – that sometimes become actual new games which rapidly replace the original version, sometimes completely rewriting the rules and producing "subversive" phenomena. Sometimes not even the game producers or owners of the server can block and remove these unforeseen parallel societies.

This recently happened to the *Sims Online* with the birth of the *Sims Shadow Government* (Nick Wadhams, *The Associated Press: Some bring Mafia attitude, tactics to online game at Star Telegram.com http://www.dfw.com/mld/dfw/news/nation/6244025.htm*, or *http://www.thesimmafia.com*).

Contemporaneously, the latest releases have softened the limits of the game space: they seem *infinite* in *Homeworld*, where the player is suspended in interstellar space, in which he can rotate 360° and change his point of view from that of one of the fighters in his fleet to the limits of outer space, from which enemy fleets are on the way to destroy his planet, in order to begin an exodus toward uncharted space. Or they can seem *indefinite*, like the beginning of *Silent Hill*, wandering through a forest that is immersed in a thick fog, where one truly has the impression of getting lost; and the closed and rigidly defined 3D labyrinth that opens out into the complexity of a city in GTA III, in which we can roam at will, listening to one of the many stations on the radio of the car we just stole, and take the wrong turn, rarely finding ourselves – according to an expert player – driving down the same street in the same situation…

> the final scene of the film, Truman is sailing his boat toward the horizon, within which he had grown up and in which day after day the

Playground 06. The Videogame and the Creation of On-line Collectivity

Opening up electronic game space within the network has lead to unexpected game environments developed by the players themselves (the mods) and the creation of an immense community that populates vast artificial and immaterial worlds, like in the Sims Online *or in* Everquest. *Beyond the codified imaginary world that these environments often reproduce, beyond the slavery to verisimilitude which is similar to that of the digital special effects in movies, it is a playground with enormous potential.*

From top to bottom and from left to right: Counter Strike, *Half Life mod,* Favela, *Brazilian mod of the same game,* Political Arena *and* Big Brother, *Quake III mod.*

The Sims Online, *Electronic Arts 2003*

events had happened implacably, regulated by a principle he can't know, but only guess at through his desire for freedom. But the horizon is a wall with sky and clouds painted on it, that stops his voyage and reveals the fiction, showing him the need: to break through the limits and open a door toward an unpredictable space, toward another story that is beginning at that very moment. (Iacovoni 2002)

We are therefore witnessing a change in videogame space: from private to public, from complicated to complex, from delimited to indefinite, in which one can begin, like in real life, not just to construct true relationships, but in which to experiment the *violation* of its rules and the spaces that form it.

But all of this is here and now, in the moment I am writing, and perhaps when you read this it will already be the past: the elements of this playground are too mobile, in constant evolution and they will probably never be even partially stabilized.

In order to project ourselves forward, therefore, we will have to look around, imagine new configurations and plot the collision routes between different media that can take videogame space one step further, out of the confines of the game, into the complexity of lived life.

OK, maybe it's clear: with a few dozen eurodollars and a telephone line you can open doors onto unpredictable spaces, where if you want you can even decide to be the bad guy, there's no danger of ending up in prison, unless you violate the copyright laws – and anyway when you're fed up all you have to do is push a button. Click. And you're somewhere else. Millions of people do it everyday: they get home, they sit down in their little corner and open a door onto the future, onto the possible. The problem is that for now it's just a bit boring: as soon as you take one step into this future there's someone who wants to beat you up, or at the most there's a little lady to pick up, and if you can't – game over. It's impossible to just take a nice walk, enjoy a beautiful sunset on a planet that's part of a solar system beyond Orion, as you discuss philosophy and exchange views with someone from over there – or is he really from Phoenix, Arizona? And you almost always find yourself in castles or spaceships you have seen hundreds of times before at the movies, or worse, you are the inhabitant of a two-story house like the ones in suburban America, and you're grown up, maybe even an architect, and so you start thinking about what a wonderful world you could build… and the worst is that you have to close yourself up in a corner of the room and get cramps in your fingers, and instead it would be nice to take these worlds around with you, let friends in, share them with your eyes open (without considering an unpleasant possibility: that you have to give those eurodollars to a multimillionaire who lives in a house that looks like the village of the Prisoner... the only thing that's missing is the white ball following the hackers around)... But then you spend hours and hours in that same little corner looking for things that are useful and important, but that are futile and fun as well, flipping through pages and pages of text that, if you're lucky, have pictures and music as well, or sometimes even going into rooms – rooms? – that have been reduced to a list of idiotic pseudonyms...

It's true, the future seems to be going in a different direction from what had been imagined: no hyperspace, no teletransporting, no immortality. And yet we have cell phones and Internet. Imagining a possible future for this playground means projecting ourselves forward ten years, no more than that. This is a relatively short period of time in the life of a human being, but it is enormous for technological evolution. It is a true gamble, almost a toss of the dice.

But a few of the trajectories are already visible: from videophones, proposing new portable devices for playing online, to three-dimensional browsers which make sharing knowledge of Internet spatial, multiplying the possibility of "visible" presences meeting up, we can start to see an extended playground joining interconnectivity, games and knowledge. The horizon could be overcoming the distinctions between (video) game space and the knowledge space mentioned by Pierre Lévy in *Collective Intelligence, for Anthropology in Cyberspace*.

> In knowledge space, the identity of the individual is organized around dynamic images, images which he produces by exploring and transforming the virtual reality he is participating in. This "virtual body" of the individual must be represented almost as though he were the animated image of his hero or his vehicle (spaceship, racecar...) in the videogame. [...] But the analogy has its limits. A videogame is supported by fixed rules, whereas an intellectual collective constantly questions the laws of its own immanent universe. A videogame is created by a programmer; but the members of an intellectual collective are them-

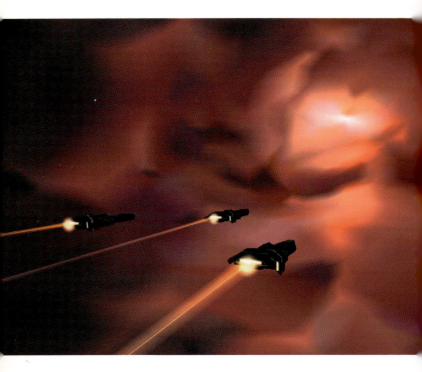

Homeworld, *Relic Entertainment, 1999.*

selves the programmers of their own universe, and also the heroes of the adventure that is unfolding within it. There is no longer a separation between the exploration and the construction of a virtual world. The videogame simulates a physical universe, whereas the intellectual collective projects a space made of meanings and knowledge. The videogame submerges the player in an imaginary *territory*, while the virtual world of an intellectual collective is a *card*, an instrument for reference and orientation which harks back to a real space, the most real space today, that of living knowledge. (Lévy 96)

After overcoming the limits of this analogy – not just the technological ones but above all those that are tied to the strictly com-

Rez, Sega, 2001.

mercial nature of videogames – a new horizon opens up into which the spaces of both game and knowledge can flow. A horizon of reflection for architecture is glimpsed which goes well beyond the pure and simple planning of the *architexture* of the games of the newest generation.

Beyond that horizon, there is the possibility of constructing a New Babylon, in the labyrinths and through the links of the web, where its presence can transform the inert, two-dimensional quality of the web page or the neutral and anonymous container of a chat room into a truly *interactive* place, one that is open to the multiple levels of communication and the construction of situations in constant change.

03: playscape

Lacerated space-time.

Dossiers to change the geography of places, spaces to conquer that are never the same in their unstable and fluctuating forms, devices to creatively overturn the social relations of space, architecture in constant transformation, that changes its skin and its structure with every change of the seasons, that moves around and forms up again according to the desires of its inhabitants, multisensorial and richly imaginative environments…

The tracks we have left in our path, that are as discontinuous as the line that connects the dots in a puzzle or the stars in the sky, draw a *playscape* that is continuously changing and constantly unrecognizable, the production and reproduction of the play of space that adapts and forms itself according to the desires of the individual and collectivity. In it, as Lefebvre writes, "the perceived, the conceived and the experienced" are superimposed; it is produced by a sort of critical *détournement* of experiences that are as distant in time as they are in substance. As mobile as the glance of each single inhabitant, they cannot be enclosed in a single point of view, nor in a recognizable configuration; it is by its very nature unrecognizable, unstable, multiple.

In this landscape, architecture as a discipline dissolves within the dynamics of real life, outside the self-referential ivory tower of language, or the *haute-couture* circuit of images. It becomes an interactive catalyst, to liberate the relationships between individuals and objects, and the other individuals, transforming itself into a device that can give its inhabitant back the power to give form, uses and meanings to things.

The goal of each one of these playgrounds, optimistically, is to influence reality with its own instruments, with an optimism that certain radical visions exaggerated in their presumption. "The very gesture of building as a means to change the world was premised upon a policy of architectural/urbanistic determinism – new spaces will in themselves produce new types of desire, new types of social relations, etc. – that seemed to ignore the materiality of power in the existent real world" (Levin 96). Plus the fact that "the social world is written in economic language" (Bourdieu 98) and that "spatiality is not only a product but also a producer and reproducer of the relations of production and domination, an instrument of both allocatable and authoritative power" (Gregory, Urry 85).

This included *New Babylon*, too, which was at least supported by an aesthetic and radical political movement that planned on changing the world. Constant declared this openly: it is a city that is planned for an inhabitant who doesn't exist yet. But many other projects, many other visions – when they weren't simply the spatialization of a new communicative dimension for the consumer society - ingenuously proposed producing new forms of collective life starting with new forms of architecture. For example, the mobile city of Yona Friedman, which guaranteed a better world generated by the increased mobility of its inhabitants.

Instead, the world that surrounds us is a sort of backwards mirror of those visions, of a *homo ludens* who has been forced by globalization to become a *homo migrans* without any accompanying technological stamp, unless one is in the business lounge of an airport, or inside a truck transporting tomatoes… a prophecy that has come strangely true, balanced between a *lie* and the imaginary, between induced stimulation of desire and its repression: a world in which functionalist theory and its opposite, play theory, both seem to have come true in a certain sense, but in a worse form than had been imagined, their exact algebraic opposite.

As Debord writes, "theories are only made to die during the war of time: these units are more or less strong and one has to

PLAYGROUND 06. BETWEEN VIDEOGAMES AND REALITY

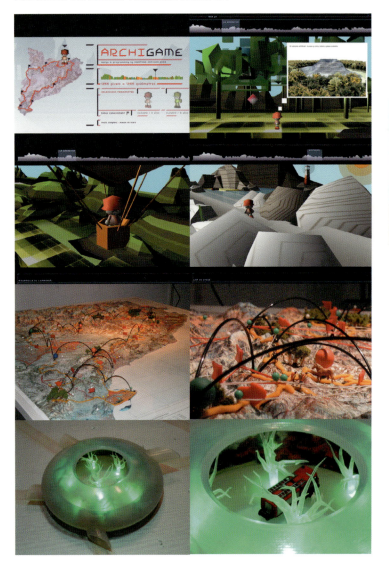

Enric Ruiz-Geli - Cloud9: HiperCatalunya, Virtual Archi-game, *2003. A new experiment to expand on-line games within the territory and vice versa.*

Superflex, Supercity, Kalrskrona 2. *"Karlskrona2 will initially be an exact replica of the city but as the virtual citizens meet and interact things will change, buildings will redefine their function, social hierarchies will alter, laws will be reconstituted and renewed. The virtual Karlskrona will be visible to the real city through a large-scale video projection in the main square. Here citizens can gather in real space to follow the activities of their avatars and consider the divergences between* Karlskrona *and* Karlskrona2" (http://www.superflex.net/tools/supercity/index.shtml).

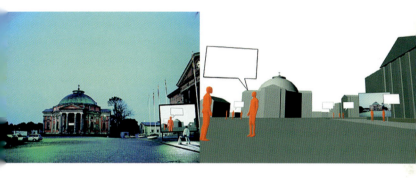

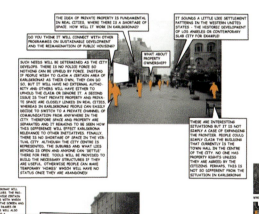

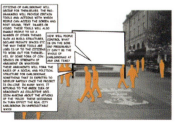

know how to use them at the right moment during the battle and, whatever their merits or shortcomings may be, one can certainly only use the ones that are there at the right time. Just like theories must be substituted, because their decisive victories – even more than their partial defeats – determine their wear and tear, no living epoch is the product of a theory: it is above all a play, a conflict, a voyage" (Debord 98).

But, *mutatis mutandis*, what is still up-to-date with those theories is the realization that architecture is an activity on the borderline between a *corresponding translation* of the dominant economic-social dynamics and the *production* of *dissimilar* spatial practices. If, during those years, there was a reaction to the ideological failure of the functional myth of the city, in search of a mental, physical and multi-sensorial space that was freed from constrictions, from the 1990's on, there was an opposite reaction to the self-referentialism of forms which had taken root during the years of disciplinary autonomy and circulation of the image. This brought architecture back within the complexity of the territory, once again expanding the field of action, in search of an operative *interstice* in which man's natural tendency to construct his own private and collective space could be turned free.

> The term *interstice* was used by Karl Marx to define the exchange communities that were escaping from the economic framework of capitalist economies, in that they were outside the laws of profit: barter, selling at a loss, autarchic production, etc. The interstice is a space in human relations which, by inserting itself more or less harmoniously and openly into the global system, offers other possibilities of exchange to those that are already working within the system. (Bourriad 2000)

In other words, if the form of a space can have an effect on the behavior and the relations between its inhabitants, by reconverting a declaration made many years ago, we could say that play architecture must liberate space from topological chains that immobilize things and men, taking a portion of space away from the socially-established order, opening a void which "can be understood with the help of the concept 'positive hole', dubbed by modern physics", in which "materializing freedom is first of all taking away from a domesticated planet a few particles of its surface" (*IS*, n. 1).

There, we could use this image taken from quantum mechanics to say that when subatomic particles manage to move through leaks and gaps in the spatial-temporal structure instantly from one position to another, and achieve a free space that lies entirely in their instability, that the playgrounds we have crossed become devices for opening and widening positive holes within social space, *zones* that are more or less *temporarily autonomous* in which they can re-acquire the indeterminate forms and functions that give the inhabitant back his appropriative and creative capacity.

But the territory is already full of holes: those zones which spontaneously, and outside the plan, produce architecture and ways to use the territory, like the *shanty towns* that are scattered just about everywhere in the so-called developing countries, or in the *terrains vagues* which can also be found in the richer cities in the rest of the world, true voids outside productive dynamics, waiting to be transformed, which Constant Nieuwenhuis himself described in a recent interview as the places where the *New Babylon* should be built today:

> Have you seen this neighborhood here in front? It was built just a short while ago, but before, when I used to work here, there used to a big *terrain vague* here with scrubland and sand… There were lots of tents, too, the nomads used to build fires, sing… for ten years I used to watch them from this window, now I have covered it up, but before it used to be open because I like watching all that. […] In the *terrain vague* everyone can do what they want. It is a Neo-Babylonian space. (Careri 2001)

This, then, is another playground, the inhabited equivalent of children's *junk playgrounds*, a low-cost and extremely successful form of playspace where "the setting is dynamic, changing as the various children add their own modifications. Cooperation in the management of material and the development of plans is necessary and projects can be progressively elaborated. In junk playgrounds children use real materials to construct their own playthings and the play occurs during the process of their building as well as in their use" (Ellis 73).

The *terrain vague* is the only spontaneous playground that, without making use of complex technology, is fluidly built through a constant negotiation of rules, limits and overlapping. It is the scene of a *play* that is sometimes conflictual, in which the inhabi-

PLAYSCAPE. THE NETWORKS BETWEEN VIRTUAL AND CONSTRUCTED SPACE

The network structures seem to have a particular capacity to generate continuous opportunities for social play, multiplying the occasions for encounter and exchange, and for the diffusion of knowledge and experiences, from Internet to the labyrinth-network of New Babylon, *passing through the dawning world of 3d browsers, from hypertext toward a possible hyperspace.*

Internet Mapping project, map of the major ISP's, http://research.lumeta.com/ches/map/gallery/index.html. *Activeworlds map August 2001,* http://activeworlds.com. *Constant,* New Babylon.

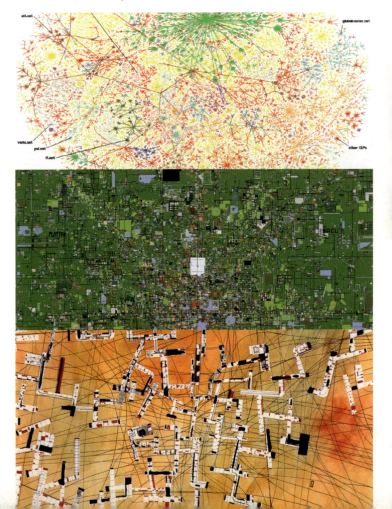

Eduardo Arroyo, NO.MAD Arquitectos, Desert City Square, Barakaldo, Spain. A park as a labyrinth, where "would-be lovers will hide on the shadow lounges or the elderly will gather around their stories, kids will play on the water ponds and skaters will keep an eye on that alternative topography." *ma0,* Carsicittà, *project for the transformation of public spaces in the Rozzol Melara neighborhood of Trieste, 2002.* Double public land is marked by an 8% network of pathways, creating a continuity and intensity of usage of the open space that was denied by the original project.

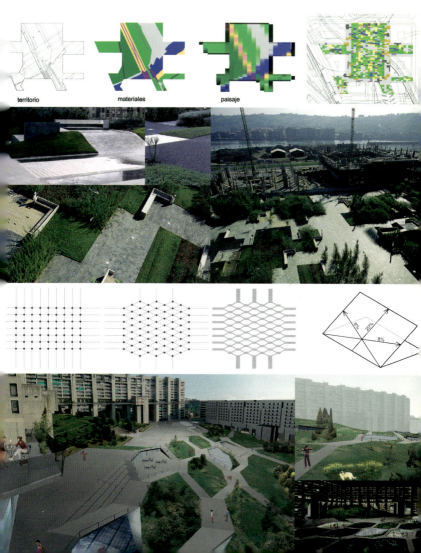

PLAYSCAPE: THE TERRAINS VAGUES

The Campo Boario is a large piazza near Rome's old town; it is part of the ex-Mattatoio complex. This area, which was abandoned years ago and never renovated, has become a terrain vague, spontaneously settled by a social center and various communities through a process of continuous renegotiation of the rules. In 1999, Stalker occupied the veterinary building along with Kurdish refugees, with the intention of creating a cultural center that was open to experimentation and cultural comparisons. They thus set off a process of direct transformation of the spaces dedicated to relations, and also called in artists and architects to partake in a continuous play.

Top: Stalker, Pranzo Boario, *1999. Bottom: Stalker,* Ararat/Campo Boario *Map 1999-2002.*

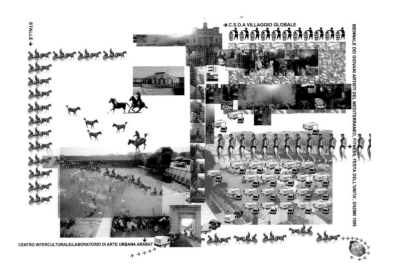

tants have become active actors in the fragile process of collective construction of public and private space.

But its limit lies in its status as a cast-off, a zone in constant movement, spurred by dynamics that are elsewhere. They are allowed a certain amount of indefiniteness in order to become land of compensation, a safety valve, while expectations are consolidated and land values rise in anticipation of a new desire to transform and integrate that space within the city.

And even if the *degrees of liberty* within it increase, the terrain vague is not a *virgin* territory hiding an authenticity of social forms and settlement potentials that are independent of the society that had produced it as a cast-off.

Each one of the playgrounds we have crossed is, on the contrary, the paradox of a project which becomes *terrain vague*, in order to overcome the unyielding contradictions between mobile and static, fluid and solid, between closed and open, limited and limitless, finite and indefinite, between orthogonal and oblique, material and immaterial, between actor and author, ethic and aesthetic, that are reproduced each time the *desires* and *needs* of a population are crystallized in a spatial form.

The goal of play architecture is to combine these opposites, going against their innate stability, solidity, closure, finiteness, aesthetic qualities, orthogonal qualities, authoritarianism, toward a molecular architecture we could define as *informal*, awaiting an inhabitant who will give it back not just its usefulness and pleasure as a function, but also its sense as a form.

The unstable balance between the celebration of spontaneity and the needs of a project, between the uncontrolled and residual play of a spontaneous city and the authoritarian and reassuring *game* of the plan, the playscape that appears on the horizon is the equivalent of an enormous *terrain vague* of meanings, uses, identity, where architecture's field of action is unfocused to the point of becoming indefinable, like the play Bateson mentioned, which cannot be enclosed within a logical category, a sort of "non" situation of some kind.

If the ultimate goal of this playscape is to give man back the right and the pleasure of molding the space he lives in, then architecture must transform itself into a continuous play which can never end. Its objective is to overcome the very contradictions that generated it, in a continuous search to do away with the distance between itself and the reality of lived life.

In other words, a *play* in which "the ultimate goal of architecture is the elimination of architecture itself" (Branzi 75).

04: playlist

This section is dedicated to listing various readings that give more in-depth knowledge of the arguments, chapter by chapter. I have tried to construct a personal *playlist*, a sort of reasoned and passionate list of texts which were fundamental to this roving "cut&paste". They have been helpful in reaching conclusions and steering a course for this navigation among experiences that are so different and distant in time.
Therefore, this is not a complete bibliography; the fact that it is only partial is in part the fault of the author's ignorance, but also of the vast quantities of experience this text is based on. We suggest, therefore, that these notes be read like the story of a personal experience, or like the *credits* of a piece of electronic music, in which the musician gives back to his authors the fragments he has used to produce, we hope, something new.

1. The Situationists

As you may have noticed by reading between the lines and paying attention to the quotes, this text owes much to the works on parabolas, from the Lettrist International to the Situationist International, where play is openly and explicitly at the center of artistic and political action. This is fundamental in order to understand its revolutionary potential, in an unpredictable encounter between aesthetics and politics.

The original texts, in the editions that were consulted:
Potlatch 96 – *Potlatch*, Gallimard, Paris 1996.
IS – *Internazionale situazionista*, Nautilus, Turin 1994.
Constant 74 – Constant, *New Babylon*, in Constant, *New Babylon Art et Utopie. Textes Situationnistes*, Jean-Clarence Lambert (ed.), Cercle D'Art, Paris 1997.
Debord, Jorn 59 – Guy-Ernest Debord, Asger Jorn, *Mémoires. Internationale Situationniste 1959*, Permild & Rosengreen; Les Belles Lettres, Paris 1993.
Vaneigem 67 – Raoul Vaneigem, *Trattato sul saper vivere ad uso delle giovani generazioni*, Malatempora, Rome 1967.
Debord 98 – Guy Debord, "*In girum imus nocte et consumimur igni*", Mondadori, Milan 1998.

The texts on Situationists:
Andreotti 96 – Libero Andreotti, *Introduction: the Urban Politics of the Internationale Situationniste*, in Libero Andreotti, Xavier Costa, *Situacionists Art, Politics, Urbanism*, MACBA ACTAR, Barcellona 1996.
Costa 96 – Xavier Costa, *Sub specie ludi*, in Libero Andreotti, Xavier Costa, *op. cit.*
Levin 96 – Thomas Y. Levin, *Geopolitics of Hibernation. The Drift of Situationist Urbanism*, in Libero Andreotti, Xavier Costa, *op. cit.*

Bandini 99 – Mirella Bandini, *L'estetico e il politico. Da Cobra all'Internazionale Situazionista 1948-1957*, Costa & Nolan, Genova 1999.
To renew the experiences and paths which lead from the ashes of surrealism to the conflictual relationship between aesthetic production and political coherence in the Internationale Situationniste. We quoted here:
Jean Baudrillard, *Per una critica dell'economia politica del segno*, Mazzotta, Milan 1974.
Wigley 98 – Mark Wigley, *Constant's* New Babylon *The Hyper-Architecture of Desire*, 010 Publishers, Rotterdam 1998 .
Careri 2001 – F.Careri, *Constant. New Babylon, una città nomade*, Testo & Immagine, Turin 2001. Return to *New Babylon* thirty years later and re-discover its relevance.

2. On Games

Bateson 77 – Gregory Bateson, *Steps to an Ecology of Mind*, University of Chicago Press, Chicago 2000.
Bateson 96 – Gregory Bateson, *Questo è un gioco*, Cortina, Milan 1996.
By combining readings from the *IS* bulletins with the many-authored reflections in *Questo è un gioco*, it was possible to establish a short circuit between play and daily existence, which was taken up again in one of the *Metaloghi* in *Verso un'ecologia della mente*. Fundamental.
Morin 74 – E. Morin, *Il paradigma perduto*, Bompiani, Milan 1974.
The explanation of the inevitable *ludens* character of the human species.
Eco 73 – Umberto Eco, Introductory essay to *Homo Ludens*, Einaudi, Turin 1973. In this critical introduction, Eco pinpoints the limits of Huizinga's text, explaining the difference between play and game.
Sartre 43 – Jean-Paul Sartre, *L'essere e il nulla*, Gallimard, Paris 1943, quoted in Martine Mauriras Bousquet, *Théorie et pratiques ludiques*, Economica, Paris 1984.
Huizinga 73 – Johan Huizinga, *Homo Ludens: A Study of the Play Element in Culture*, J. & J. Harper Editions, New York 1970.
It is quoted everywhere, but one has to wonder just how many people have actually read it. The title is worth the entire book.
Giorgio Agamben, *Infanzia e storia*, Einaudi, Turin, 1979.
Breton 66 – André Breton, *Manifesti del surrealismo*, Einaudi, Torino 1966.
The importance of surrealism in our research lies completely in this sentence: "The urgent need we feel to stop with the old antinomies like action and dream, past and future, reason and madness, high and low, etc. forces us to not spare the one about serious and non-serious (play), which in turn commands the one of work and leisure, 'wisdom' and 'foolishness', etc."
About real playgrounds:
Ellis 73 – Michael J. Ellis, *Why People Play*, Prentice-Hall Inc., Englewood Cliffs, N.J. 1973.

3. …and other things

Sacks 98 – Oliver Sacks, , *The Man Who Mistook His Wife for a Hat and Other Clinical Tales*, Simon & Schuster, New York 1998. Comical and dramatic cases but illuminating concerning disturbances of perception.
Lefebvre 81 – Henry Lefebvre, *La production de l'espace*, Editions Anthropos, Paris 1981
Sennet 98 – Richard Sennet, *The Conscience of the Eye. The Design and Social Life of Cities*, Norton, New York 1992.
Bourdieu 98 – Pierre Bourdieu, "A reasoned Utopia and Economic Fatalism", in *New Left Review*, no. 227, 1998.
Gregory, Urry 85 – D. Gregory, J. Urry, Social Relations and Spatial Structures, Macmillan, London 1985.
La Cecla 88 – Franco La Cecla, *Perdersi. L'uomo senza ambiente*, Laterza, Bari 1988.
Serres 72 – Michel Serres, "J'habite une multiplicité d'espaces", in *L'interference*, Minuit, Paris 1972.
Bourrriaud 2000 – Nicolas Bourriaud, *Esthétique relationelle*, Les presses du réel, Paris 2000.
Bey 97 – Hakim Bey, *Zone temporaneamente autonome*, Shake, Milan 1997.
Alberto Iacovoni, Bring the noise, in *http://architettura.supereva.it/collection/20011216/index.htm*.
Alberto Iacovoni, *Omini. Pretesto per una playlist collettiva*, in *http://architettura. supereva.it/books/scelti/2002120701/index.htm*.
Two reflections on the meaning of collage and sampling in architecture.

4. The Radicals

By intertwining the Situationist play with general reflections on games and space, a short circuit is created which can extend itself to experiences that aren't declaredly associated with play, like radical experiences. A true goldmine of information to help understand the cultural climate of those years can be found in the architectural magazines of those years, and in particular the section "News and Comments" of *Casabella*, which was edited by Mendini in the early 1970's. There, one can find Branzi's "Radical Notes", along with comments by other exponents of that multiform phenomenon. The contemporary section "Cosmorama" of *AD - Architectural Design* is also important and closer to the future experiences that would be set off by the visions of Archigram.

Luigi Prestinenza Puglisi, *This is Tomorrow*, Testo & Immagine srl, Turin 1999. To help orient oneself among the thousand facets of radical architecture of the 60's and 70's.

Orlandoni, Vallino 77 – Bruno Orlandoni, Giorgio Vallino, *Dalla città al cucchiaio. Saggi sulle nuove avanguardie nell'architettura e nel design*, Cooperativa Editoriale Studio Forma, 1977 Turin. The essay in the *Trigon 69* catalog is quoted, *Trigon 69*, Graz 1969. A merciless analysis of the radical phenomenon, it in fact, condemns it as decadent mannerism, lucid, but probably the result of a critical attitude that was organic to the left-leaning Italian culture of those years…
Toraldo di Francia 2001 – Cristiano Toraldo di Francia, *Superstudio & Radicaux*, in *Architecture radicale*, Institut d'art contemporain, Villeurbanne 2001.
Feuerstein 2001 – Gunther Feuerstein, *L'architecture visionnaire en Autriche*, in *Architecture radicale*, Institut d'art contemporain, Villeurbanne 2001.
Branzi 75 – Ugo La Pietra, *I gradi di libertà*, Jabik & Colophon, Milan 1975.
Coop Himmelblau 66 – Coop Himmelblau, "L'architecture des nuages", in *Architecture-Principe 1966 et 1996. Paul Virilio et Claude Parent*, Les Editions de l'Imprimeur, Paris 1996 .
Archigram 91 – *Archigram*, Birkhauser, Basel 1991.
Curtis 99 – Barry Curtis, *A Necessary Irritant*, in Dennis Crompton (ed.), *Concerning Archigram*, Archigram Archives 1999.
Banham 76 – Reyner Banham, *Megastructure. Urban Futures of the Recent Past*, Thames and Hudson, London 1976.
Marie Ange Brayer, *La ville des cartes habitées. Mobilité et migration dans l'architecture des années 1950-60 dans la collection du FRAC Centre*, in *http://www.frac-centre.asso.fr/public/collecti/textes/crit01fr.htm*

5. Videogames and Cyberspace

Literature about videogames is expanding well beyond the already boundless market of magazines for players; it now offers critical approaches that can analyze its qualities as a communicative media and expressive form with aesthetic qualities. The network is obviously one of the most widespread, easily-accessed basins in this continuously evolving panorama.

D'Alessandro 2002 – Jaime D'Alessandro, Personale storia dei videogame in 24.000 caratteri, in *PLAY: il mondo dei videogames*, catalogue, Edizioni Palazzo delle Esposizioni, Rome 2002.
Iacovoni 2002 – Alberto Iacovoni, *Lost in Space, breve storia dello spazio nei videogiochi*, in *PLAY: il mondo dei videogames*, catalogue, Edizioni Palazzo delle Esposizioni, Rome 2002.
Iacovoni 2003 – Alberto Iacovoni, *Space Invaders, il futuro è sempre dall'altra parte*, in Marco Brizzi, Paola Giaconia, *INTIMACY*, Mandragora, Florence 2003.
Lucien King, *Game On: The History and Culture of Videogames*, Laurence King Publishing Ltd, London 2002.

Bits Generation 2000 "TV-games", catalog of the exhibit at the Kobe Fashion Musem/TV Game Museum, Kobe 2000.

Steven Poole, Trigger Happy, *Videogames and the Entertainment Revolution*, Fourth Estate, London 2001.

Noah Falstein, *Portrait of the Artists in a Young Industry*, in *http://www.theinspiracy.com/ArPAYSIG.htm*.

Zimmerman 99 – Eric Zimmerman, in *If/Then 1.0: PLAY*, Netherlands Design Institute, Rotterdam 1999

J.C. Herz, *Gaming and the Art of Innovation. Doors of Perception 7: Flow*, in *http://flow.doorsofperception.com/content/herz_trans.html*.

Graeme Murrell, *A Drifters Guide to Physical and Virtual Urban Space, Monocular Texts*, in *http://www.monoculartimes.co.uk/texts/architexts/driftersguide1.shtml*.

Nick Wadhams, T*he Associated Press: Some Bring Mafia Attitude, Tactics to Online Game on Star Telegram.com*, in *http://www.dfw.com/mld/dfw/news/nation/6244025.htm*, or go directly to *http://www.thesimmafia.com*.

Lévy 94 – Pierre Lévy, *L'intelligenza collettiva. Per un'antropologia del cyberspazio*, Feltrinelli, Milan 1996.

The Information Technology Revolution in Architecture is a new series reflecting on the effects the virtual dimension is having on architects and architecture in general. Each volume will examine a single topic, highlighting the essential aspects and exploring their relevance for the architects of today.

Other titles in this series:

Information Architecture
Basis and Future of CAAD
Gerhard Schmitt
ISBN 3-7643-6092-5

New Wombs
Electronic Bodies and Architectural Disorders
Maria Luisa Palumbo
ISBN 3-7643-6294-4

HyperArchitecture
Spaces in the Electronic Age
Luigi Prestinenza Puglisi
ISBN 3-7643-6093-3

New Flatness
Surface Tension in Digital Architecture
Alicia Imperiale
ISBN 3-7643-6295-2

Digital Eisenman
An Office of the Electronic Era
Luca Galofaro
ISBN 3-7643-6094-1

Digital Design
New Frontiers for the Objects
Paolo Martegani /
Riccardo Montenegro
ISBN 3-7643-6296-0

Digital Stories
The Poetics of Communication
Maia Engeli
ISBN 3-7643-6175-1

The Architecture of Intelligence
Derrick de Kerckhove
ISBN 3-7643-6451-3

Virtual Terragni
CAAD in Historical and Critical Research
Mirko Galli / Claudia Mühlhoff
ISBN 3-7643-6174-3

Advanced Technologies
Building in the Computer Age
Valerio Travi
ISBN 3-7643-6450-5

Natural Born CAADesigners
Young American Architects
Christian Pongratz /
Maria Rita Perbellini
ISBN 3-7643-6246-4

Aesthetics of Total Serialism
Contemporary Research
from Music to Architecture
Markus Bandur
ISBN 3-7643-6449-1

Light Architecture
New Edge City
Gianni Ranaulo
ISBN 3-7643-6564-1

History of Form*Z
Pierluigi Serraino
ISBN 3-7643-6563-3

Digital Gehry
Material Resistance /
Digital Construction
Bruce Lindsey
ISBN 3-7643-6562-5

Flying Dutchmen
Motion in Architecture
Kari Jormakka
ISBN 3-7643-6639-7

Induction Design
A Method for Evolutionary Design
Makoto Sei Watanabe
ISBN 3-7643-6641-9

Behind the Scenes
Avant-garde Technologies
in Contemporary Design
Francesco De Luca / Marco Nardini
ISBN 3-7643-6737-7

The Charter of Zurich
De Kerckhove Eisenman Saggio
Furio Barzon
ISBN 3-7643-6735-0

New Scapes
Territories of Complexity
Paola Gregory
ISBN 3-7643-6736-9

Hyperbodies
Toward an E-motive Architecture
Kaas Oosterhuis
ISBN 3-7643-6969-8

Digital Odyssey
A New Voyage in the Mediterranean
lan+
ISBN 3-7643-6970-1

Mathland
From Flatland to Hypersurfaces
Michele Emmer
ISBN 3-7643-0149-X